RIVER THAME

history & guide

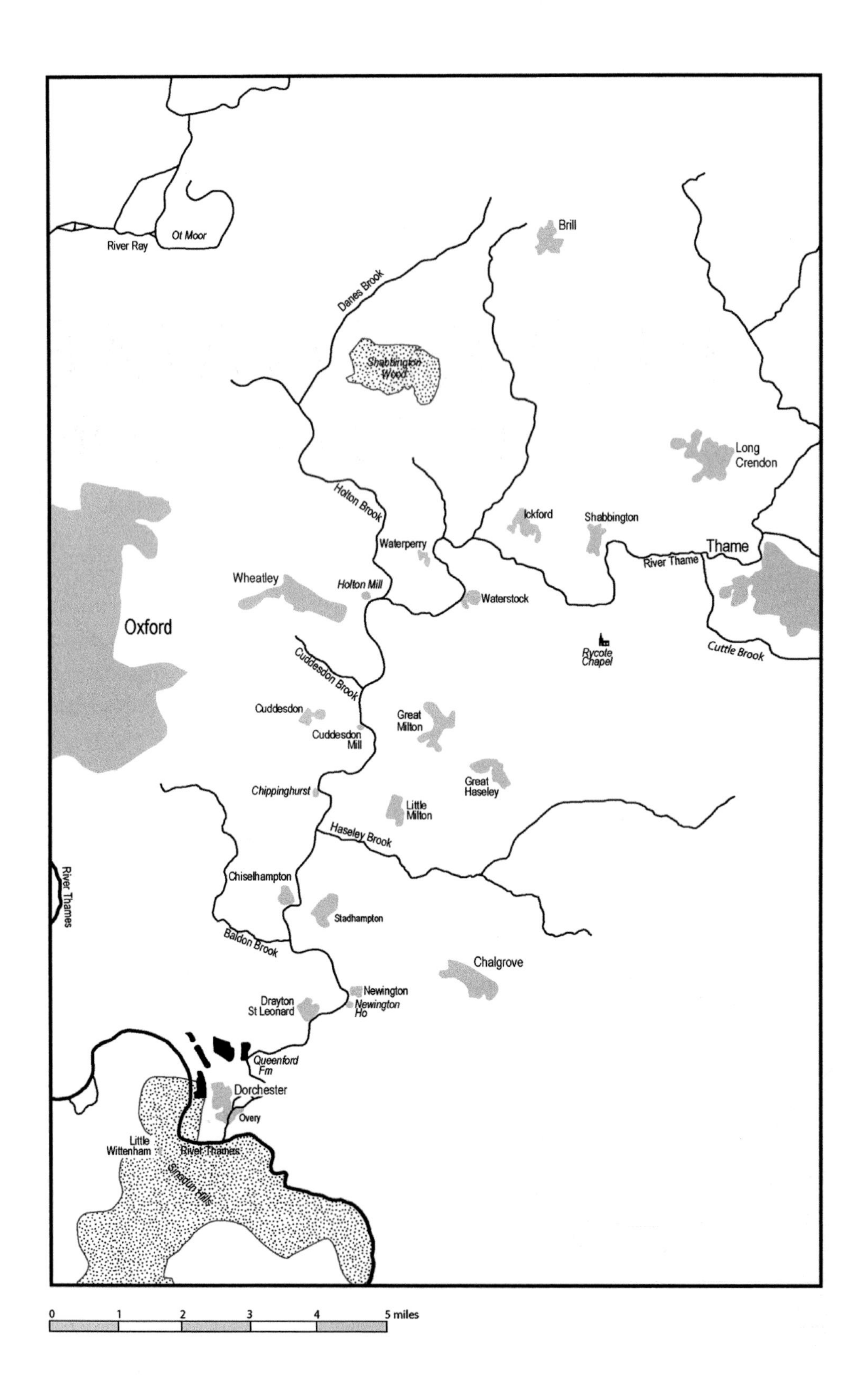
River Ray
Ot Moor
Brill
Danes Brook
Shabbington Wood
Long Crendon
Holton Brook
Ickford
Shabbington
Waterperry
Thame
River Thame
Wheatley
Holton Mill
Waterstock
Oxford
Rycote Chapel
Cuttle Brook
Cuddesdon Brook
Cuddesdon
Great Milton
Cuddesdon Mill
Great Haseley
Chippinghurst
Little Milton
Haseley Brook
River Thames
Chiselhampton
Stadhampton
Baldon Brook
Chalgrove
Newington
Drayton St Leonard
Newington Ho
Queenford Fm
Dorchester
Overy
Little Wittenham
River Thames
Sinodun Hills
0
1
2
3
4
5 miles

RIVER THAME
OLD CHILTERN'S SON

history & guide

Tony Chaplin

TEMPUS

Frontispiece: Map showing towns and villages in the proximity of the River Thame and its main tributaries, from Thame to Dorchester. (A map showing the river from source to Thame can be found on page 20.)

First published 2007

Tempus Publishing Limited
The Mill, Brimscombe Port,
Stroud, Gloucestershire, GL5 2QG
www.tempus-publishing.com

British Library Cataloguing in Publication Data.
A catalogue record for this book is available from the British Library.

ISBN 978 0 7524 4373 7

Typesetting and origination by Tempus Publishing Limited
Printed in Great Britain

Contents

	Preface	6
	Acknowledgements	8
	Introduction	9
one	From Source to Aylesbury	19
two	Aylesbury to Chearsley	32
three	Notley to Thame	45
four	Thame	57
five	Shabbington to Waterstock	71
six	Wheatley to Chippinghurst	84
seven	Chiselhampton to Drayton St Leonard	96
eight	Queenford to Dorchester	105
nine	Walking Tour	117
	References	120
	Bibliography	123
	Index	126

Preface

This is the story of a river, its places and people, its past and present. The Thame is only a small river, even by British standards, running a mere forty miles from its source in the foothills of the Chilterns to its confluence in Oxfordshire with the Thames, which is by comparison some 215 miles from beginning to end and thus the longest wholly English river. From a global perspective, even the Thames is small. Ronald Carton, the first and longest-serving editor of *The Times* crossword puzzle, wrote that:

> We English cannot boast about the greatness of our rivers – that is, about their greatness measured coldly in miles either of length or width. Nor do we. We do not seek to match our Thames with Amazon, our Mersey with Mississippi, our Severn with Zambezi. These could swallow our rivers, hardly accounting them rivers, almost our country even and scarcely know the difference. We have no imposing deltas, no thunderous cataracts, no perilous rapids. But if they are no giants, our rivers have personality and character. They are very much a part of our lives, almost of ourselves.

This is surely as true for the Thame as for the Thames or any other British river.

As we shall discover shortly, our title has its source in the poetic imagery of the seventeenth century English poet Michael Drayton, one of a number of writers through the centuries to draw inspiration from the personality and character of this delightful little river that flows across the heart of our country. The Thame still holds the same appeal that so fascinated those writers of bygone years. It has its own story to tell, and that is what we set out to explore.

John Taylor, a contemporary of Drayton, wrote a description of the Thame and Oxford's Isis that he claimed included, 'all the flats, shoares, shelves, sands, weares, stops, rivers, brooks, bournes, streames, rills, rivulets, creeks, and whatever helps the said rivers have, from their springs or heads, to their falls into the ocean'.

What follows is not intended to be a fully comprehensive, encyclopaedic account in this way, but rather a compilation of personally chosen snapshots of times, places and people that in different ways reflect the life of the river and its environs. Nor is there likely to be anything startlingly new to some readers, but rather a gathering together of the familiar and sometimes, hopefully, the less familiar, of *miscellanea* that for one reason or another appealed to the author. Hopefully there is usually at least some tenuous link to the river, if only geographic proximity, though some details

River Thame at Ickford Bridge.

unearthed in the course of delving really have no connection at all to the river and therefore should have no place in the main text.

For example, it may be of little interest to most, but was rather more so for the writer, to discover that the letter bearing the very first Penny Black adhesive postage stamp, issued in May 1840, was posted to a certain George Waterman at an address in Thame. Or that when the great preacher John Wesley addressed an assembly in an upper room at a property in Thame in 1778, so great was the throng that the floor allegedly collapsed under the weight! Actually, the extent to which this story is true is uncertain. Another contemporary account suggests that some of the floor was deliberately removed to allow the crowd downstairs to hear Wesley's sermon. Maybe the latter action precipitated the former calamity. Maybe the story is entirely apocryphal. Whatever the 'truth', the two reports epitomise a problem that seems to crop up with frustrating regularity, a problem that is doubtless no different in our own times, namely, the reliability of different people's perceptions and accounts of the same incident, and the modifications that occur with the passage of time. Clearly, much that has been passed down to us is not primary evidence; often such material is sadly lacking, and we are left to make our own best judgment.

The research has entailed a steep learning curve for one woefully ignorant of so many aspects of our history, of natural history and the making of the landscape, of architecture, and of a whole spectrum of other topics. It has nonetheless been a most fascinating experience, and it is sincerely hoped that readers will in some measure be able to share the delights of this little voyage of discovery.

Acknowledgements

In compiling this text, I have drawn heavily on information contained in many other writings, and the referenced works are listed in a rather substantial bibliography at the end of the book. Two other sources of information have also proved most useful, but their individual components are too numerous to list in detail. Firstly, I have enjoyed gathering and reading the booklets and leaflets produced by a whole range of towns, villages, churches, councils and other organisations in the area along the course of the river, and have profited greatly from them. I readily acknowledge their usefulness and thank their authors, who in many cases are anonymous. Secondly, I have benefited equally from tapping into the vast mass of data available on the internet, and indeed, have found the challenge of seeking information in this way to be quite rewarding in itself. I am aware that some such data is often unsubstantiated, and may indeed be conflicting, but where I am as satisfied as I can reasonably be as to the validity of the information, and have eventually quoted directly from these sources, I have included the website address in the bibliography.

I am grateful to the following individuals and organisations for permission to reproduce illustrations from their collections: Jean and Keith McCullagh; Juan Piris; All Souls College, Oxford; Buckinghamshire County Museum; English Heritage; the Hurst Water Meadow Trust; the Oxfordshire County Council Photographic Archive; the Record Office for Leicestershire, Leicester & Rutland; the *Thame Gazette*. Helene Beard provided invaluable help with the preparation of the maps and other illustrations. Some of the unascribed illustrations are of unknown provenance; a number are photographs by Rachel Chaplin, whom I thank; the remainder are my own.

It gives me great pleasure to acknowledge a number of individuals who have assisted in various other ways. Stephen Bending, from the University of Southampton, was most helpful with his comprehensive advice concerning the works of some of the Early English writers. My friends Shirley Fox, Pam Killick, and Jane Goldsmith, read preliminary drafts of the text, and were able both to highlight errors and to make suggestions as to how the manuscript might be improved. I am truly appreciative of their comments and encouragement, and hope that the finished product fulfils their earlier confidence; any residual inaccuracies are entirely of my making. Finally, I am indebted to Nicola Guy and Claire Forbes at Tempus Publishing Ltd for their enthusiasm for this submission, and subsequently for patiently and expertly guiding me through the editorial and publishing process.

Introduction

Though (for the most part) in the tracts I tread,
Of learned Camden, Speed and Hollinshead,
And Draytons painfull Polyolbyon,
Whose fame shall live, despight oblivion,
These are the guides I follow, with pretence
T'abbreviate and extract their quint-essence.
(J. Taylor)

The fourteenth and fifteenth centuries have come to be regarded as the great age of exploration. The culmination of a series of social, political and technological awakenings led to a widening of our British and European forebears' horizons and a desire to venture from the known world into uncharted territory. We too are embarking on a modest voyage of discovery, but our own journey along the River Thame is rather different in a number ways, not least in that we know where we are heading, even though, as we shall see shortly, our starting point is rather less certain. We have at our disposal sophisticated maps and countless guidebooks to lead us on our way, rather than hand-drawn charts or spoken descriptions that may lack authenticity or reliability. We have at our fingertips the latest high-tech satellite navigation and imaging aids to plan and direct our journey, rather than sun or stars that may, or may not, be visible. Yet instead of all this, we begin by taking a bird's eye view of our route by means of the writings of the English historian Raphael Holinshed, *c.* 1529-1580.

Holinshed's main work, *Chronicles of Englande, Scotlande, and Irelande*, was published in 1577/78 and later revised by his collaborators and re-published after his death. The *Chronicles* was used as a major source by many Elizabethan dramatists and is thought, for example, to be the inspiration for a number of Shakespeare's historical plays, such as *Hamlet* and *Macbeth*. In our own times it has little credence as an accurate, historical account, being considered a blend of fact and legend, though some would argue that it is nonetheless a vital record of how Elizabethans perceived and recorded their world. Its description of the River Thame (actually in a section of the *Chronicles* now thought to have been written by William Harrison) defines the context of our journey along the river and is intrinsically interesting for its listing of the place names in the area, albeit as spelt in the late sixteenth century:

> Thame riuer riseth in the easterlie parts of Chilterne hils, towards Penleie parke, at a towne called Tring west of the said parke, which is seauen miles from the stone bridge, that is betweene Querendon and Ailsburie (after the course of the water) as Leland hath set downe. Running therefore by long Merston, and Puttenham, Hucket, and Bearton, it receiueth soone after a rill that commeth by Querendon from Hardwike, and yer long an other on the other side that riseth aboue Windouer in the Chilterne, and passing by Halton, Weston, Turrill, Broughton, and Ailsburie, it falleth into the Tame west of the said towne (except my memorie doo faile me.) From this confluence the Tame goeth by Ethorpe, the Winchingtons, Coddington, Chersleie, Notleie abbeie: and comming almost to Tame, it receiueth one water from southeast aboue the said towne, and another also from the same quarter beneath the towne; so that Tame standeth inuironed vpon thrée sides with thrée seuerall waters, as maie be easilie séene. The first of these commeth from the Chiltern east of Below or Bledlow, from whence it goeth to Hinton, Horsenden, Kingseie, Towseie, and so into the Tame. The other descendeth also from the Chilterne, and going by Chinner, Crowell, Siddenham, and Tame parke, it falleth in the end into Tame water, and then they procéed togither as one by Shabbington, Ricot parke, Dracot, Waterstoke, Milton, Cuddesdon, and Chiselton. Here also it taketh in another water from by-east, whose head commeth from Chilterne hils, not farre from Stocking church, in the waie from Oxford to London. From whence it runneth to Weston (and méeting beneath Cuxham with Watlington rill) it goeth on to Chalgraue, Stadham, and so into the Tame. From hence our streame of Thame runneth to Newenton, Draton, Dorchester (sometime a bishops see, and a noble citie) and so into the Thames, which hasteth in like sort to Bensington, Crowmarsh, or Wallingford, where it receiueth the Blaue, descending from Blaueburg, now Blewberie, as I learne.[1]

Holinshed (or Harrison) seems to interchange the spelling of Tame and Thame quite randomly. The name Thame is generally thought to be of Celtic origin, and shares its root word *tamesa* with other river names: the Tame in Staffordshire, that from Tudor times powered water hammers for iron forges, and gives its name to the town Tamworth; the Tame, separating Cheshire from Lancashire, and flowing from the foot of the Pennines to the tidal Mersey; the River Teme, the second largest tributary of the River Severn, that flows from the Kerry Hills in mid-Wales towards Worcester; the Team, a tributary that flows into the Tyne near Dunston Coal Staithes, the largest wooden structure in Europe, possibly the world; the River Tamar, that forms the border between much of Devon and Cornwall and flows through a valley designated an Area of Outstanding Natural Beauty; and of course, the mighty Thames itself, about which countless books have been written, flowing through the extremes of rural and industrial landscape, past humble homes and seats of royal and political power. The town of Thame, like Tamworth above, takes its name from the river on which it stands, and having a Celtic name is thereby distinct from many of the towns and villages in its locality that generally bear Anglo-Saxon names. Such places often have names ending in -ton (such as Shabbington), -den (Cuddesden), -ham (Haddenham), -worth (Marsworth), or -wick (Hardwick).

Etymologists such as Eilert Ekwall, a great authority on place names, suggest a parallel between the Celtic *tamesa* and the Sanskrit word *tamasa*, meaning 'dark river' or 'dark water', and speculate that the word spread from India through the Celts to Britain. As Sanskrit and the Celtic language are both Indo-European languages, the proposition seems not unreasonable. There is a river actually called Tamasa; it is a tributary of the Ganges, and rises some 2,000 feet above sea level in the Kaumur Hills in North Central India. Curiously, Thame is the name of a secluded Nepalese village in the foothills of Mount Everest. Lying a mere 12,467 feet above sea level amidst spectacular scenery on the old salt trade route between Tibet, Nepal and India, it is well known to Everest trekkers and even boasts its own monastery. It was, by the way, the childhood home of Tenzing Norgay, the Sherpa who accompanied John Hunt on that first much acclaimed conquest of Everest in 1953, and is presently home to another Sherpa who has now reached the summit of Everest on a remarkable ten occasions.

The Celtic (Brythonic) word from which Thame is derived means 'gently flowing' and for the greater part this is a most apt description of the River Thame, since it falls only about 164 feet in the course of its journey to the Thames at Dorchester, running generally westward through a broad, flat flood plain and surrounding water meadows to the west of Aylesbury in Buckinghamshire and later into Oxfordshire.

Herein, perhaps, lies the rural charm that was certainly of appeal to writers of bygone years, and before we embark on our little journey, we pause for a moment to consider some of these literary works. The late sixteenth and seventeenth century continued to be a time of great curiosity about exploration at home as well as the far-flung places of the world, and topographical writing was much in vogue. As well as Holinshed's *Chronicles* and the rather more factual travelogues of John Leland, to which we will refer later, writers such as William Camden and Edmund Spenser wrote eloquently and fancifully in the course of some of their more substantial works, of rivers such as the Thame, and their surroundings. In these works, as we shall see, rivers and other features of the landscape are often personified with human characteristics and relationships, with frequent emphasis on love and marriage.

Camden (1551-1623) was himself a much-travelled Elizabethan scholar, historian and antiquary, and published in 1586, in Latin, his *Marriage of Thame and Isis* as part of a greater work *Britannia*, a blend of narrative and verse. In *Britannia* he often seems to pursue his journey by following the courses of rivers rather than roads. His words certainly add a different perspective to our view of the countryside, as he describes the Thame in candid terms as a bride, eagerly awaiting and preparing for marriage to her beloved:

> Meanwhile, gliding out of the Chiltern hills, Thame eagerly drank in the fires of the bridegroom she longed for. Frustrated at her lack of acquaintance with his bed and intent on the marriage, she hastened her steps, and for her the lengthy days seemed to stand still, until in her eagerness she could place her name before that of her lover.

> What mortal deeds does eagerness not compel? Now she left the village known by their name, repeating "good-bye, farewell" to the Norrises. At length ancient Dorchester was espied, bringing an augury of the sought-for marriage. Then Thame reappeared, having bound her hair with ears of corn, clad in a green robe, surpassing the fingers of Aurora and the countenance of Dione. The roses of Paestum did not rival her lips, nor jewels her eyes, nor lilies her tresses, nor snow her neck. And as she flowed she pushed her dripping tresses over her back, and imposed order and shape on her waving hair. And lo, Isis suddenly raised his brow above his peaceful waters, and through all the fields the golden beams of his dripping face shone bright. Now he joined many kisses with his hoped-for Thame, they enfolded each other's necks with embraces, a thousand kisses could be heard, their arms grew pale from embracing, their lips joined their spirits. At length they went down together to their marriage-bed, where holy Concord, joined with Faith, sanctified their splendid wedding with their solemn words.[2]

We noted above that the original is in Latin, and there is a degree of variation, even paraphrase, in the translations that are available, though the overall theme remains the same. Some may prefer the rather more literal, explicit translation of Dr Edmund Gibson in 1722:

Now had fair Tame sigh'd for her promis'd spouse,
While down the Cateuchianian hills she flows,
And scarce saluting her old banks runs by,
Bearing no load, but long virginity:
And this she seems ambitious to lay down,
And see her lover's stream augmented by her own.
With a faint kiss she mocks the walls of Tame,
And leaves behind her nothing but her name.
Yet tho' impatient Isis arms to fill,
She stops to bid the Norrises farewel.
Old Dorchester stands wondring at her speed,
And gladly bids the happy match suceed.

Now does the joyful Bride new drest appear,
Fresh blades of Corn tye up her golden hair,
Her shining gown plays with the purled air.
Blushing Aurora to her hand gives place,
Nor proud Dione boasts so fair a face.
Her lips the rose, her eyes bright gems outdo,
Her hair the lilies, and her skin the snow.
In state she swims, her careful hand throws back
Her floating tresses on her silver neck.

Proud Isis now his comely head displays,
And cheers the drooping fields with golden rays.
Nor stays he to admire his Tama's charms,
But throws himself (sweet load!) betwixt her arms.
Ten thousand kisses do ten thousand meet,
And with their breath the Lovers souls unite.
Hence to their bed the happy pair go down,
Where Faith and Concord speak them into one.[3]

There was no such potential ambiguity in translation when some ten years later, Edmund Spenser (1552–1599) published, in English, his monumental work *The Faerie Queene*. Spenser was well connected and counted men such as Sir Walter Raleigh among his acquaintances, but was to die in penury even though, according to his memorial in Westminster Abbey, he was regarded as, 'The Prince of Poets in his Tyme'.

One section of *The Faerie Queene* describes how the rivers of the world come to the hall of Proteus, the Greek god regarded as shepherd of creatures of the sea, for the marriage of the Thames and the Medway. Amidst lists of the great and distant rivers of the world, he honours the little old River Thame as being father of the Thames:

But him before there went, as best became,
His ancient parents, namely th'ancient Thame.
But much more aged was his wife than he,
The Ouze, whom men do Isis rightly name.
...But Thame was stronger, and of better stay;
Yet seemed full ancient by his outward sight,
With head all hoary, and his beard all gray,
Dewed with silver drops, that trickled down always.[4]

Note the change of gender – for Camden the Thame is female (the bride), for Spenser the Thame is male (the groom's father). In *Polyolbion,* another work from the same era, Michael Drayton also describes the Thame in male terms, though this time as the groom himself:

Now fame had through this isle divulged in every ear,
The long-expected day of marriage to be near,
That Isis, Cotswold's heir, long woo'd was lastly won
And instantly should wed with Thame, old Chiltern's son.
And now that woodman's wife, the mother of the flood,
The rich and goodly vale of Aylesbury, that stood
So much upon her Thame, was busied in her bowers,

Preparing for her son, as many suits of flowers,
As Cotswold for the bride, his Isis, lately made;
Who for the lovely Thame, her bridegroom, only stayed.[5]

Drayton (1563-1631), a friend of Camden and Ben Jonson, was a most prolific poet of religious, historical, topographical and pastoral verse, and *Polyolbion* (1622) is regarded by many as his masterpiece. It is not his only work to mention the Thame, however, and in *Idea* (XXXII To the River Anker) published in 1619, he briefly describes how 'Cotswold commends her Isis to the Thame …'.[6] We should perhaps briefly comment on the use of the name 'Isis'. Isis, the name given to the Thames about Oxford, has little to do with the Greek goddess of that name, and is more likely derived from the Celtic word *uisge*, meaning water, that is also the root word from which the rivers Ouse, Usk and Exe take their names. Camden suggested that the Thame and Isis, 'mix their names as well as their waters, being henceforth call'd Tham-Isis or the Thames'.[7] The Romans called the Thames Tamesis, the spelling 'Thames' gradually evolving during the Norman period, and it is now mostly regarded as little more than literary conceit to assume that England's most famous river takes its name as Camden supposes.

We opened this chapter with a brief, but characteristic example of the doggerel that was the hallmark of John Taylor (1580-1653), the self-styled 'Water Poet', a man who was familiar with both the Thame and the Isis, and a contemporary of Drayton. He was a flamboyant character, a Thames ferryman (or wherryman) by trade, yet something of a minor celebrity, who enjoyed the patronage of Ben Jonson and members of the royal court. He was a true Royalist, and went with the court to Oxford at the beginning of the Civil War, during which period he wrote as a pamphleteer of Royalist propaganda. In his time he was also a 'bottleman' (an excise officer who collected duty for the Governor of the Tower of London on wine imported through the city) and, rather unsuccessfully, an alehouse keeper. He ended his days in poverty, however, and may even have died of starvation.

Well known in his younger days for his rollicking verse and prose, Taylor achieved further notoriety by nearly drowning in the course of an attempt to sail down the Thames from London to Queenborough on the Isle of Sheppey. Nothing particularly remarkable about that, readers may be thinking, except that he undertook the forty-mile excursion in a boat constructed of brown paper, kept afloat with bullocks' bladders, and powered by oars made of dried fish tied to canes. Little wonder that while Taylor paddled, his companion on the trip prayed, or that on the return journey, he remarks, 'we hied us home on horseback all in post'.[8]

In view of his first hand experiences, Taylor was perhaps, or perhaps not, better qualified than others to write of rivers and the like. One of his poems, *Thame-Isis*, was written in 1632 and includes a description of the union at Dorchester of the Isis and the Thame, a confluence that seemed to fascinate so many writers around this time:

... Attend Dame Isis downe to Dorchester,
Neare which the lovely Tame doth meet with her.
There Tame his Isis doeth embrace and kisse,
Both joyn'd in one, cal'd Tame or Tamesis ...

Tame doth derive his spring or pedigree
Neare Marworth in the Vale of Aylsbury
From where he many miles with strange meanders,
To find his lovely Isis slowly wanders.

Through fertile lands a quiet course he keeps,
Till southward under Whatley bridge he creeps,
And (like a pilgrim) travels all alone
No Brooke or River waiting him upon,
Only three namelesse Rivolets and two Springs
Which very privately their tribute bring ...
Whil'st th'eddies divers wayes doth turne and trace,
Tame doth with Isis dance the wilde goose chace.[9]

Later lines are rather less flattering of the Thame:

Poor Thame all heavy and disconsolate,
Unnavigable, scorned, despised, disgraced ...
He hurls himself into Isis arms.[10]

Hardly the romantic notion that some of our other writers have portrayed, but then Taylor described a picture, a situation or a person just as he saw it. Cromwell, his political opposite, once instructed his portrait painter, the Dutch artist Peter Lely, to paint him, 'warts and everything as you see me',[11] without ostentation or concealment of any blemish. Taylor was perhaps more of this inclination than were his Royalist associates, who generally went to great pains to create the right impression and appearance.

We turn now to writing intended perhaps for a rather different type of audience, for anyone, in fact, regardless of status or politics, sharing the same common interest. *The Compleat Angler*, written originally by Izaac Walton (1593-1683), though later enlarged with contributions from Charles Cotton, was first published in 1653. It was not the first such work, and certainly not the last. An earlier, anonymous book on angling, *A Treatise of Fishing with an Angle,* predates Walton's effort by more than 150 years, but after the *Bible* and the *Complete Works of Shakespeare, The Compleat Angler* is arguably now the most published book in the English language. It is a discursive, rambling, and at times whimsical work, that sets out to show that there is more to angling than simply hooking some poor, unfortunate fish, but praise indeed that our little river is deserving of mention, albeit again in connection with the greater Thames. In his discussion concerning British rivers, Walton writes, 'The chief is THAMISIS, compounded of two rivers, Thame and Isis; whereof the former, rising somewhat beyond Thame in Buckinghamshire, and the latter near Cirencester in Gloucestershire, meet together about Dorchester in Oxfordshire; the issue of which happy conjunction is Thamisis, or Thames'.[12]

Still we see the lingering notion concerning the derivation of the name Thames. Later, in praise of that mighty river, he picks up the idea again:

Such streams, Rome's yellow Tiber cannot show,
The Iberian Tagus, or Ligurian Po:
The Maese, the Danube, and the Rhine,
Are puddle-water all, compared with thine:
And Loire's pure streams yet too polluted are
With thine much purer to compare;
The rapid Garonne, and the winding Seine,
Are both too mean,
Beloved Dove, with thee
To vie priority;
Nay, Thame and Isis when conjoin'd, submit
And lay their trophies at thy silver feet.

The work is a rather curious blend of folklore, literature, song and verse, with personal reminiscences of rural life, all interspersed among practical advice for anglers. One poem commended, and possibly even commissioned by the authors, is entitled *Angler's Song*. It was written by a little-known poet William Basse (almost a fishy pun to be made there!) who lived at Moreton, a mile or so from Thame, and who had been educated at Lord Williams's School, Thame, of which more later. While extolling the merits of angling, it has to be conceded that the poem is hardly classic verse, as the opening lines reveal:

As inward love breeds outward talk,
The hound some praise, and some the hawk.
Some, better pleas'd with private sport,
Use tennis, some a mistress court:
But these delights I neither wish
Nor envy, while I freely fish.[13]

For our final selection of glimpses of the Thame from literature of earlier years, we move on to some better-known writers from the eighteenth century. Matthew Prior (1664-1721) was both a poet and a diplomat. His poem *Henry and Emma*, a sentimental burlesque of an old fifteenth-century ballad entitled *The Nut Brown*

Maid, was allegedly written in 1708 whilst sitting under an oak tree at Wittenham Clumps, close to the spot where the Thame joins the Thames:

Where beauteous Isis and her Husband Tame
With mingl'd Waves, for ever, flow the Same:
In Times of Yore, an ancient Baron liv'd;
Great Gifts bestow'd, and great Respect receiv'd.[14]

Around the same time, another English poet was beginning to make his mark. Like Prior, whose father was a Dorset joiner, Alexander Pope (1688-1744), the son of a draper, came from relatively humble beginnings. Childhood illness impeded both his growth and his education, and he was consequently largely self-taught. It was something of a triumph over adversity, therefore, that, unlike some of the other writers and poets we have mentioned, he enjoyed lifelong financial security following his translation of Homer's *Iliad*, a task that took him several years starting from 1715. A while before this greater prosperity he had written, in 1709, a poem entitled *Summer, The Second Pastoral, or Alexis* in which he writes:

A shepherd's boy (he seeks no better name)
Led forth his flocks along the silver Thame,
Where dancing sunbeams on the waters play'd,
And verdant alders form'd a quivering shade.[15]

Later, in Windsor Forest (1713), in a section describing the River Thames, he again briefly mentions the Thame in positive tone:

Around his throne the sea-born brothers stood;
Who swell with tributary urns his flood:-
First the famed authors of his ancient name,
The winding Isis and the fruitful Thame!
The Kennet swift, for silver eels renowned;
The Loddon slow, with verdant alders crowned;
Cole, whose dark streams his flowery islands lave;
And chalky Wey that rolls a milky wave;
The blue transparent Vaudalis appears;
The gulphy Lee his sedgy tresses rears;
And sullen Mole that hides his diving flood;
And silent Darent stained with Danish blood.[16]

It was a rich era for creative writing, but Daniel Defoe (1660-1731), a contemporary of both Prior and Pope, and probably best known for his *Robinson Crusoe*, was seemingly scornful of some of his predecessors' works when writing a few years after our excerpts from Pope were published. In *A tour thro' the whole island of Great Britain, divided into circuits or journeys*, vol. 1 (1724), he declares in his description of the Thames:

> I shall sing you no songs here of the river in the first person of a water-nymph, a goddess, and I know not what, according to the humour of the ancient poets; I shall talk nothing of the marriage of old Isis, the male river, with the beautiful Thame, the female river (a whimsey as simple as the subject was empty); but I shall speak of the river as occasion presents, as it really is made glorious by the splendour of its shores, gilded with noble palaces, strong fortifications, large hospitals, and public buildings; with the greatest bridge, and the greatest city in the world, made famous by the opulence of its merchants, the increase and extensiveness of its commerce; by its invincible navies, and by the innumerable fleets of ships sailing upon it to and from all parts of the world.[17]

At another point in the same work, he expands his case, claiming that the majority of writers favour his view:

> From Thame, a great corn market, the Thame joins the other branch call'd also the Thames, at a little town call'd Dorchester. I observe that most of our historians reject the notion that Mr. Cambden makes so many flourishes about, of the marriage of Thame and Isis; that this little river was call'd the Thame, and the other, the Isis; and that being join'd, they obtain'd the united name of Thamisis: I say they reject it, and so do I.

Perhaps at Defoe's prompting, we should draw a curtain over any further discussion of these Early English literary masters and move on to consider our river in a rather more factual way, with less of the romantic notions evident in those sixteenth and seventeenth-century writings. We will visit the towns and villages through which it passes, meet some of its people, and enjoy the countryside that is the Thame Valley. As a reminder of our route, each of the succeeding chapters commences with a brief extract from the passage by Holinshed to which we referred earlier; we should note that for some reason, he does not mention Wheatley, preferring instead nearby Milton as the more significant location.

one

From Source to Aylesbury

Thame riuer riseth in the easterlie parts of Chilterne hils ...

The River Thame begins its life not from a single spring but from two groups of streams, rising to the north and east of Aylesbury, that converge just to the north-west of the town. One writer has described it as the, 'harvest of many small streams',[18] though these tiny waterways are too numerous to mention individually – many are unnamed anyway – and no one of them is consistently regarded as the definitive source of the eventual river. Many accord that privilege to a stream arising near Marsworth; some regard Thistlebrook, rising near Mentmore, as the principal; others one near Wilstone.

Earlier we mentioned John Leland (spelt on his gravestone as Leyland, *c.* 1506-1552), the famous antiquary and topographer. The last five years of his life were a struggle with mental illness, and he was certified insane in 1550, a condition that persisted until his death. In his younger and healthier days, and particularly over the period 1535-1543, he travelled widely by royal commission through England and Wales on a fact-finding tour. His resulting work, *Itinerary,* is an unique, and often the earliest, record of places in England and Wales at the end of the Middle Ages and the start of the Reformation, and was a reference work for many subsequent writers. We will refer frequently to his authoritative writing. On the subject of the source of the Thame, however, even Leland is somewhat vague, 'Tame Rivar selfe, as I there lerned, rysethe in the ester parts of all the Chilterne Hilles toward Dunestaple, and the hede of it by estimation is about 7 miles from Stonebridge, on Tame, betwixt Querendune and Aillesbyri'.[19]

Defoe is little more precise as to his perception of the source of the river, and further confuses the issue unnecessarily with his interchange of the spelling of the names 'Tame', 'Thame' and 'Thames', even though we know, from comments that we noted in the previous chapter, that he was aware of the distinction between the two rivers. He writes:

We went on from Aylesbury to Thame or Tame, a large market town on the River Thames: This brings me to mention again The Vale of Aylesbury; which as I noted before, is eminent for the richest land, and perhaps the richest graziers in England: But it is more particularly famous for the head of the River Thame or Thames, which rises in this vale near a market town call'd Tring, and waters the whole vale either by itself or the several streams which run into it, and when it comes to the town of Tame, is a good large river.[20]

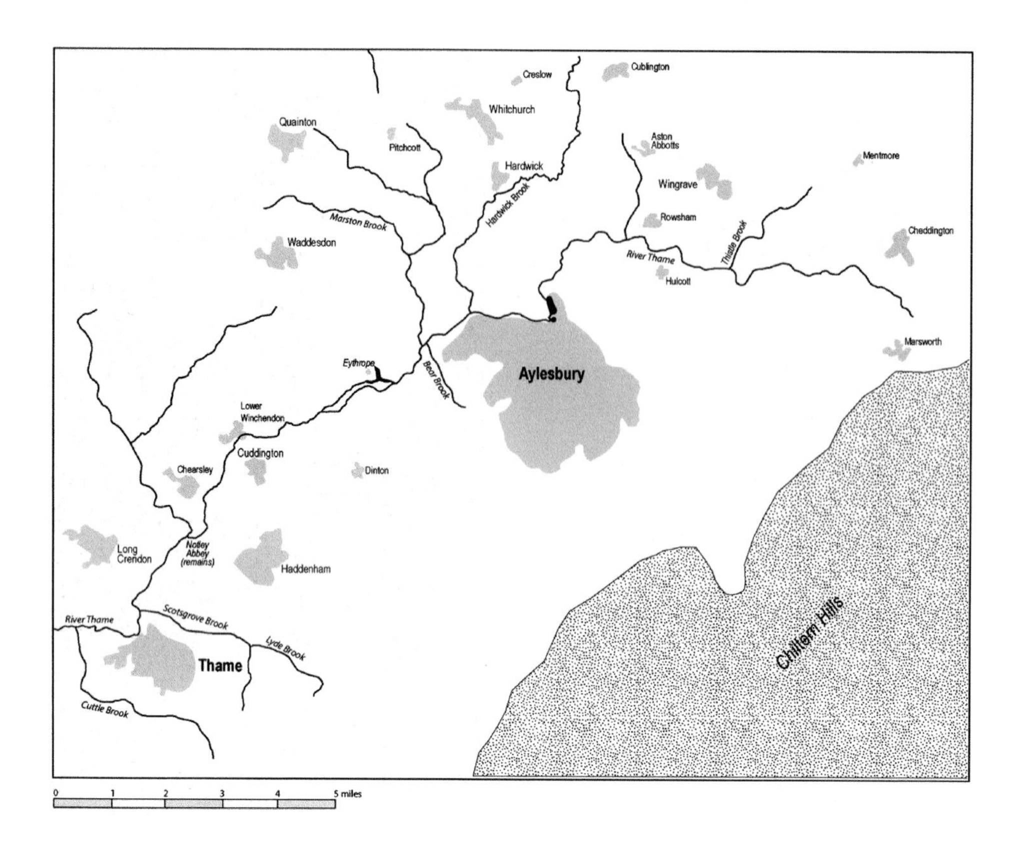

Certainly it is the amalgamation of streams from the eastern group, rising in the foothills of the Chilterns, that, downstream from Rowsham and well before Aylesbury, merits description on Ordnance Survey maps as the River Thame. These feeder streams, modest as they may be in themselves, pass several features of interest to students of the landscape and its history, and it is perhaps worthwhile considering their general significance, as some of them will be encountered from time to time in the course of our journey along the Thame.

One of the main branches of the eastern arm arises a little to the south of the village of Cheddington. At the time of the Domesday Book, the record commissioned by William the Conqueror to find out exactly what his newly acquired territory of England was worth, Cheddington was known as Cetendone, meaning 'Cetta's hill'. The stream that eventually forms part of the Thame makes its way past two hills on which is lingering evidence of a series of terraces or lynchets, the remnants of some ancient farmers' labours. The word 'lynchet' (sometimes linch or linchet) is derived from the same old English root word *hlinc*, meaning terrace or ridge, from which our modern coastal 'links' golf courses take their name. Lynchets originated from a time when hillside fields were ploughed horizontally, with unploughed strips left at intervals, a practice that goes back to the time of Alfred the Great, possibly even earlier. The way the land was actually ploughed led to the soil being turned to the

Opposite: Map showing towns and villages in the proximity of the River Thame and its main tributaries, from its sources to Thame.

Right: A bust of John Leland, once in All Souls College, Oxford. (Reproduced with the permission of the Warden and Fellows of All Souls College, Oxford, from William Huddersford's *Life of John Leland* 1772)

lower side, so that over a period of time, the downward trend of the earth changed the hillside strips into terraces. As well as the lynchets, there is some indication of a hill fort on South End Hill, possibly dating from the Iron Age. In spite of its ancient heritage, Cheddington had to wait a long time for 'fame'. When it came it was both sudden and unexpected, for the village was catapulted to national prominence in August 1963, when the Royal Mail's Glasgow to London Travelling Post Office train was stopped by tampered signals near to the village, and robbed of about £2.6 million in an audacious crime to be known forever more as the Great Train Robbery.

Meanwhile, Thistlebrook, the other, slightly more northerly branch of the eastern arm of the Thame, itself an accumulation of tiny streams, and perhaps a leading contender as the precursive river, is scarcely more than a mile or so into its course when it passes close to Tiscott deserted village earthworks. Many 'shrunken' or 'deserted' sites, such as Tiscott, are thought to date from the medieval period, particularly from times when the population fell dramatically as climatic conditions deteriorated and the country was afflicted by endemic disease such as the Black Death. At Tiscott, earthworks reveal evidence of a sunken way (the track way through the village) and house platforms (where buildings once stood). Nearby fields reveal ridge and furrow formations. These are derived from another technique used in ploughing the narrow strips of land that was the norm from as far back as the Middle Ages, and are visible at several points along the full course of the Thame.

Medieval farming was in many ways surprisingly sophisticated. Use of land and rotation of crops depended very much on the way land was divided up amongst the farmers. The basic unit of land was a selion; two or three selions constituted a strip, several strips were aggregated into a furlong (originally a measure of area, rather than length), and furlongs into fields. A selion was usually 220 yards (a furlong) by eleven yards (or two rods), equalling half an acre. Ridge and furrow came naturally from driving an asymmetrical mouldboard plough, usually pulled by four pairs of oxen, within the narrow limits of a selion. The natural action of the plough threw the soil to the right, thus forming a ridge along the central line of the selion. Over several seasons, the ridge thus formed would get higher, and the furrow would go deeper. What we now see as the undulating, corrugated formation of ridge and furrow is a field that has not been ploughed since the medieval technique was in use.

Often the selions and strips would develop curved ends, because of the tendency of the plough team to pull to the left in preparation for making the turn at the end of the strip, thus creating the overall shape of an elongated reverse 'S'. We shall see later how this phenomenon can be preserved today even in an urban layout.

As an aside to this brief diversion from our journey along the Thame, it is interesting to note that a furlong (furrow length) was measured as the distance a team of oxen could pull the plough before stopping for a breather. Similarly, an acre was at one time defined as the area that could be ploughed by one team of oxen in a day. Clearly this was not an exact science, as these measures would depend on the nature of the soil, the stamina of the oxen, and other local conditions. How many readers remember those exercise books that had a host of weights and measures on the back cover, and recall pondering the mystery of those redundant terms rod, pole and perch? The explanation has its origins with the farmers of this era. Whilst a medieval ploughman handled the actual plough, his 'boy' controlled the oxen by means of a stick, long enough to reach the farthest animal in the team. This was a rod (or pole or perch) and measured about sixteen and a half feet, or five and a half yards. It too was a somewhat arbitrary measure, but assumed a far more scientific basis in the sixteenth century when, allegedly, a rod was lawfully defined as the combined length of the left feet of sixteen men as they left church on a Sunday morning! On that pious note, perhaps we should leave ridge and furrow, rods and furlongs, and go down to the river once more.

A little further on from Tiscott, Thistlebrook is joined by the Cheddington stream and passes close to the village of Hulcott (hovel cottages). There is some evidence, if only from the name, of a settlement here dating back to Celtic times, perhaps related to proximity to the nearby ford at Thistlebrook. Whatever its earlier history, by around 1600 a substantial village had grown up, including a church and manorial complex. As well as the house, the latter included a moat, fishponds, a watermill and a windmill, and for now we will look briefly into the significance of two of these features of medieval life.

Although originally moats had been used as a means of defence of castles and other substantial and important buildings, their use gradually extended to the property of the gentry and then of more prosperous farmers, becoming something of a status symbol of the times and a reflection of man's constant striving for self-improvement, as well as a defence against unwanted visitors, whether animal or human. Your average farmer might not be able to boast battlements around his roof, or be able to afford the latest high-tech plough, but he was able dig a moat to show that he was keeping up with, or even a bit ahead of the Joneses! Consequently moats, whether grandiose, water-filled structures, or simple, dry ditches, were employed around not just castles, churches and monasteries, but also ordinary houses, gardens and even haystacks. Remnants of moats are therefore rather more common than might be expected from perceptions based on their generally grand portrayal by film-makers in modern times.

Fishponds on the other hand, really were more likely to be the prerogative of the wealthy, and remained so until their eventual decline. The Middle Ages has been described as 'the golden age of fish',[21] for fish was a significant component of the diet, and a ready source of fresh food, valued particularly during Lent when eating of meat was forbidden by the church. Consequently, fish farming was extensively developed by this time, though it was to decline in popularity after the dissolution of the monasteries. It was widespread in royal residences as well as monasteries (kings were said to be particularly partial to pike and bream) and also associated with the dwellings of nobility and gentry. There is clear evidence of a range of sophistication in technique, ranging from relatively simple 'stew-ponds' to quite complex hatcheries, that was presumably a reflection of the social standing of the owner. The more elaborate constructions comprised a system of channels, dams and sluices running from one pond to another, with each pond devoted to one stage of the life cycle of the fish; proximity to a river was clearly an advantage.

But back for the moment to Hulcott. A former vicar in the village had, in his younger days as a curate in Yorkshire, acted as matchmaker and later officiated at the wedding of Maria Branwell and Patrick Brontë. The rest, as they say, is history, and Revd William Morgan, perhaps quite rightly, claimed to have been instrumental in initiating and solemnising a marriage that in due course gave birth to the literary genius of the Brontë sisters. The church is probably little changed from his day, and Thistlebrook borders the parish now as then.

Hulcott, or Hulcote as it was once known, also provides our first encounter with a family that had enormous influence in and around Buckinghamshire for many generations. Sir Robert Lee of Hulcote, who died in 1616 (the same year as Shakespeare) is remembered not only at Hulcott, but also by memorials at Hardwick, where he owned land, and, with other members of his family, at St Mary's church in Aylesbury. He was a cousin to Sir Antony Lee of Quarrendon, father of Sir Henry Lee, both of whom we shall encounter shortly. It is believed that the extended Buckinghamshire Lee family were ancestors of Henry 'Light-Horse

Harry' Lee (1756-1818), an American Revolutionary cavalry officer, whose son General Robert E. Lee (1807-1870), the famous Confederate Leader, won several major battles during the American Civil War (1861-1865) before his eventual defeat at Gettysburg and final surrender to General Grant at Appomattox in 1865. It is one of those curious quirks of history that these namesakes and descendents of the Lee dynasty were themselves to make history on a continent of which their Tudor English forebears were scarcely aware.

A few more turns in Thistlebrook and it passes just to the south of Rowsham, a small village dating from Anglo-Saxon times, with a name meaning 'Hrothwulf's home', and recorded in 1170 as Rollesham. Once there was a ford over Thistlebrook on the old road from Hulcott to Rowsham, but historically, the more significant links have been with Wingrave, in which parish it lies. At one time Rowsham could claim a little chapel of its own – St Lawrence's, a chapel of ease – but this was dismantled in the sixteenth century, whereas the village's small defunct brewing industry is at least remembered by local place and street names. Nowadays, the A418 Aylesbury to Wing road divides the village in two, and inconspicuously crosses Thistlebrook, or the River Thame, as seamlessly it is soon to become. Shortly past Rowsham, a little stream joins the larger one. It has flowed from Aston Abbotts, once the country seat of the Abbotts of St Albans, and more recently the home of the famous polar explorer and discover of the North Pole, Sir James Clark Ross (1800-1862), and through Burston, also known in medieval times as Bricstock, or Birdstane, where the famous Lee family had one of their several homes.

And so, after a somewhat convoluted journey that is typical of the whole course of this river, the Thame finally arrives at Aylesbury, where it skirts an area now known as Watermead. This housing development was built in the late 1980s on farmland that formed part of the floodplain of the River Thame. Although it is only a small river, its character changes significantly following heavy rainfall, as is evidenced by an extensive and at times spectacular floodplain. The river has a catchment area that stretches across three counties, Buckinghamshire, Oxfordshire and Hertfordshire, with surface run-off contributing the majority of input to the main river. Permission for the development at Watermead was granted only on condition that suitable alternative flood contingency plans were provided. Consequently, the design incorporated a large lake capable of taking excess water when the river level was high, by means of gated inlets and outlets at the north and south ends, and a low meadow, now often used as a launch site for hot-air balloons, but designed to hold excess water at peak times. The lake itself is some thirty feet deep at its centre, and initially took three days to fill with water from the Thame. It has become a popular spot, both for fishermen, and for a variety of waterfowl – and the children armed with bags of bread with which to feed them (the ducks, that is!).

A little further on, just past the Aylesbury United football ground that, ironically, around the time of writing was used briefly for 'home' fixtures by Thame United, the River Thame is crossed by the A413 Buckingham Road at Holman's Bridge. Today,

Feeding time for waterfowl at Watermead, Aylesbury.

the bridge is a brick structure with five round arches, not unattractive when viewed from the riverbank, but a structure of the same name was in existence here in 1554, being mentioned in a charter from that time when Aylesbury was granted borough status as a reward for supporting Mary Tudor's accession. It was this 'Charter of Incorporation' that entitled the borough to elect two representatives to Parliament. In modern times, the bridge, being flat at road level, is inconspicuous to those travelling over it and easily overlooked, but in earlier years it was clearly a strategic crossing point of the river and the marshy ground adjacent to it. At the time of the Civil War (1642–1651), Aylesbury was consistently a supporter of Parliamentarianism in spite of the determined efforts of Prince Rupert and his Cavaliers based at Oxford to regain it for the King, and on 1 November 1642, Holman's Bridge was reputed to be the site of a battle between the forces of Prince Rupert, the King's nephew, and Sir William Balfour.

Balfour was heavily outnumbered, but the men of Aylesbury formed a militia, which attacked the Royalists from behind. A contemporary account describes a 'happy and glorious victory' for Balfour, who in spite of being outnumbered in the main battle, 'sent at least 200 of (Prince Rupert's) men to salute the earth, never more to rise hence',[22] and then allegedly killed 600 more as, aided by his local supporters, Balfour chased the Royalists out of town. In 1818 large quantities of human bones were found nearby in pits four to five feet deep, and were thought to be relics of

Statue of John Hampden in Market Square, Aylesbury.

the battle. At the instigation of the distinguished historian Lord Nugent, at that time MP for Aylesbury, they were moved to a communal grave in the churchyard at Hardwick, in whose parish they had been found. Recently uncovered evidence suggests that the Battle of Holman's Bridge was little more than a skirmish, with few casualties, but begs the question, therefore: who then are the 247 persons now buried at Hardwick? We probably now will never know whether they were indeed 'friend and foe, united in the soil which bred them'.[23]

Contrary to some reports, it seems probable that John Hampden, who came from a family of wealthy landowners who lived at nearby Great Hampden, was not present to support Balfour at Holman's Bridge. Nonetheless, a bronze statue in Market Square in Aylesbury, that does credit Hampden with involvement in the battle, affirms and commemorates his status as a local hero. Later we shall look more closely at a little more of his direct influence on the instigation and course of the Civil War.

Whether the Battle of Holman's Bridge was a full-scale battle or simply a lively skirmish, one that did survive was the Mad Hatter of Holman's Bridge. Real name Roger Crab, it is said his wits became addled after his skull was split during the battle. After running amok, he was sentenced to death by Cromwell, but later pardoned. He opened a hat shop in Chesham, where he grew increasingly more eccentric, boasting that anyone could survive on three farthings a day, and living on water, turnips and grass. Recognising his extreme unpopularity, and following a spell in the stocks, he moved on to Uxbridge where he styled himself as 'The English Hermit – Wonder of the Age'. Doubtless his bizarre life would have been forgotten in time had not Lewis Carroll chanced upon the tale and immortalised The Hatter in his *Alice* adventures.

But we should return to our own story. From Holman's Bridge, the Thame flows westward across the north of Aylesbury towards the A41 Bicester Road, accompanied now by the recently developed Aylesbury Riverside Walk pathway. The walk has areas of meadow and woodland and boasts snipe, reed bunting and linnet among its residents. Swan and moorhen are also to be seen, though in some places it is difficult to see quite how they find a way through dense reeds and bulrushes. Sadly, particularly near the bridges at either end of the walk, the detritus of human intervention is all too obvious, with the occasional shopping trolley or traffic cone, not to mention tin cans and plastic bags and bottles, discarded casually into already naturally congested water.

The pathway is sandwiched between the river and firstly the Meadowcroft estate and then Quarrendon, a large housing area that came into being after the Second World War, and named after the ancient village of Quarrendon (Querendone or Cweorndun, meaning 'hill where querns [mill-stones] are obtained', which is to the north just across the river. Quarrendon was clearly known to Leland for he describes how in the course of his travels he, ' … passed a little NNW from Tame church over Carenton [Crendon] bridge, of four stone arches; and hence by some hilly, and afterwards great pasture grounds, fruitfull of beanes, ten miles to Querendon, in the Vale of Aylesbury, where Mr. Antony Lee dwelleth'. [24]

Antony Lee, who died around 1550, was the father of Sir Henry Lee, whom we will mention again shortly. Antony's wife, formerly Lady Margaret Wyatt, was a childhood friend and later trusted lady-in-waiting to Anne Boleyn, and attended the ill-fated queen on the scaffold. After a final speech protesting her innocence, Anne pressed her prayer book into Lady Margaret's hands and stepped forward to be executed. In 'her little prayer book, set in gold enamelled black which she [Lady Margaret] long preserved as a precious relic', [25] Anne had written a farewell message to her faithful friend, 'Remember me when you do pray, that hope doth lead from day to day'. [26] Lady Margaret was later depicted in the allegorical nursery rhyme, *London Bridge is broken down* (as distinct from the more commonly known *London Bridge is falling down*), the second line of each of the eleven stanzas repeating the phrase 'Dance over my Lady Lee'. [27] The rhyme depicts the rise and fall of the generally unpopular Anne Boleyn, who is clearly identified as the unnamed central character of the rhyme 'the gay ladye', by virtue of direct reference to her confidante Lady Lee.

Antony Lee's family lived at Quarrendon Manor for over 250 years from about 1499 when Richard Lee obtained the lease after the property had reverted to the Crown, though Lees, notably one Benedict Lee, had been farming there from much earlier in that century. In those 250 years, the Lees managed to advance from yeoman graziers to peers of the realm, and Quarrendon was just one of Sir Henry Lee's houses in Buckinghamshire and north Oxfordshire.

There is evidence that the original village dates back considerably further than the time of the Lees of Quarrendon – certainly as far as the Anglo-Saxon period – for it was the place where the English saint Oswyth was born and probably raised. In adult life she established a convent at Chich in Essex, where she was later murdered by marauding Vikings in AD 653 after refusing to renounce her Christian faith. Earlier events in her life, including near death by accidental drowning when still a child, possibly even in the Thame, seem difficult to substantiate, and perhaps belong to legend. At the time of the Domesday Book, Quarrendon Manor was held by Geoffrey de Mandeville, whose son, also a Geoffrey, enjoyed great wealth and influence during the reign of King Stephen (1135-1154), though he is remembered chiefly for his treachery and violence at the time of the brutal power struggle between Stephen and Henry I's daughter, the empress Matilda.

The de Mandevilles owned other estates around the Home Counties, one of which was at what is now known as Stoke Mandeville, another village close to Aylesbury. A dispute in the seventeenth century over taxes relating to this same property, by then owned by the Hampden family, acted as the catalyst that plunged the country into civil war on an altogether greater scale than that experienced in Stephen and Matilda's day.

The ancient village site at Quarrendon is now designated a Scheduled Ancient Monument (SAM), and includes remnants of the medieval village, and the site of a sixteenth-century manor house and formal gardens. Nearby are the remains of St Peter's chapel, a chapel of ease, constructed for the convenience of those unable to get to the main church of the parish, in this case St Mary's in Aylesbury. It was built around 1280 but allowed to fall into disrepair early in the nineteenth century, some of the stone being used to repair other local buildings. All that now remains are portions of some outer walls, plus evidence of a moat and fishponds.

Perhaps Sir Henry Lee (1533-1611), who owned much of the land in the area, including Quarrendon, Pitchcott and Oving, was accustomed to using the chapel when in residence at Quarrendon Manor. In his youth he had been a courtier to Henry VIII; he was later knighted and became a favourite of Queen Elizabeth I, whom he entertained at the Manor in 1592. As well as his status as Master of the Leash and Master of the Armoury, Sir Henry enjoyed great personal skill and success at tilting, and he originated and for some thirty years supervised the annual Accession Day Tilts and other extravaganzas held to celebrate Elizabeth's accession to the throne, and to personally fulfil a vow to uphold the Queen's honour against all comers. It is thought that he was the inspiration for Walter Scott's 'Queen's Champion' in his novel *Woodstock*.

It was not only titles and accolades that he gained during his time at Court, however, for Sir Henry also acquired a mistress, or 'reading lady',[28] as she was politely known. Anne Vavasour herself had apparently had a succession of lovers, but after

Sir Henry's wife died in 1590, went to live with him at Ditchley until his own death. This did not please his beloved Queen, though she did relent and visited the couple in 1592.

Sir Henry had been brought up in the household of his uncle, Sir Thomas Wyatt (1503-42), who himself spent most of his relatively brief life in the service of Henry VIII. From time to time, Sir Thomas fell out of favour with the King, most notably, perhaps, when he was imprisoned in the Tower of London under suspicion of being one of Anne Boleyn's lovers. He was, above all, a distinguished poet in his day, the first writer of sonnets in English, and considered by many to be one of the first writers of the English Renaissance. Not surprisingly, in years to follow, Sir Henry Lee was regarded as one of the most cultivated men in the Queen's Court, and was said himself to be something of a poet. A beautiful song, commencing, 'His golden lockes Time hath to silver turn'd' (still performed in our contemporary repertoire of Baroque music) comes at the end of a longer poem, *Polyhymnia*, a work written by George Peele, *c.* 1558-1597 and performed in 1590 to commemorate Sir Henry's retirement from the office of Queen's Champion. Some claim the song to be the work of Sir Henry himself; the closing stanza would certainly reflect his unswerving devotion to Elizabeth, 'Goddess, allow this aged man his right To be your beadsman[29] now that was your knight'.[30]

Perhaps his own privileged education accounted for Sir Henry's advanced ideas about education – he was the founder of Aylesbury Free School. But there was yet one further side to his accomplishments; Sir Henry was evidently also a most successful farmer, even though on at least one occasion he was made painfully aware of the vagaries of farming in such low-lying land. Large banks had been built to protect the Manor and the chapel from flooding, but neighbouring farmland was clearly more difficult to protect from the elements. The great storm of 1570, the so-called 'All Saint's Day Flood', was so destructive at Quarrendon that Sir Henry is said to have lost 3,000 sheep, not to mention horses and cattle. In spite of the protective measures, the chapel also was damaged to an extent that, of necessity, Sir Henry subsequently 'renued the Ruines of this Chapell'.[31]

The Quarrendon SAM also includes the site of a medieval rabbit warren. It is estimated that there could still be as many as 2,000 of these artificial warrens, sometimes called 'pillow mounds', remaining around the country. For instance, there are said to be at least twelve in Blenheim Park, not so many miles away from the Thame. Rabbits were introduced into the country in Norman times as a source of both food and fur. They were far less robust creatures than those of our own day, and needed to be fed and provided with protection, both from the elements and from predators. Artificial warrens were built consisting of low flat-topped mounds, sometimes with stone-lined burrows, and often surrounded by a shallow ditch to prevent escape, as rabbits do not like to swim! The animals would be fed through the winter and then cropped the following year. Throughput of rabbits was such that the larger warrens would constitute a significant component of the local economy.

Close to these medieval and Elizabethan artefacts at Quarrendon are some other earthworks, presumed to be of Civil War origin, possibly Parliamentarian batteries or the site of a minor skirmish. However, no factual evidence has been unearthed to support such claims, and their true nature will probably never now be known. Running through the area is the single stream, derived from the northern group of mostly unnamed streams and brooks, including those arising near Durton and Stewkley, that have been gradually merging and meandering southward, past the village of Hardwick with its 247 unexplained bodies, on to Aylesbury and a final confluence with the Thame, not far from the Bicester Road.

Many of the little watercourses that run from the north towards Aylesbury and the Thame meander through villages and countryside whose very existence was threatened in the late nineteen-sixties and early seventies by the prospect of making way for London's third airport. Cublington, close to one of these streams running towards the Thame, was one of the doomed villages threatened with obliteration. John Betjeman (1906–1984) once suggested that this little community, 'with its red brick and thatch, is the sort of village one would give a prize to as undisturbed England'.[32] And undisturbed it remained, for a massive campaign 'Wings Off Wing' averted the threat to the area, and instead, the complex at Heathrow was expanded. The former Second World War RAF airfield at Cublington, near Wing, is now a chicken farm, though the layout of the runways can still be made out from the air. At the time of the Norman Conquest, the village was known as Coblincote, but by about 1400, the original village had been abandoned and a new settlement developed on the present site, slightly higher up the hill. Now all that remains of the old village is the Beacon, a mound on which once stood a motte and bailey castle, and remnants of a medieval graveyard, designated an Ancient Monument. Just south-west of the village, the stream is crossed by a simple bridge that bears an inscription, set rather inconspicuously, almost at road level, indicating the way to Aston Abbotts and Whitchurch.

By now, the stream has gathered others arising across the Vale of Aylesbury. One comes from the curiously elongated village of Stewkley, with its Norman church and profusion of medieval carvings. The village was known in Norman times as Stiuclai, so called from the stiff-clay of its soil, and was once intriguingly described as, 'a village that is not noticeably connected with the rest of the world'.[33] Another headstream arises near Littlecote, and yet another starts its life in the famous meadow land of Creslow, where sheep and cattle were grazed for kings and queens, and where now stands the oldest inhabited dwelling in Buckinghamshire. The growing stream flows on past Hardwick, in whose fourteenth-century church is a monument to Sir Robert Lee, and then is joined by another brook that springs from Whitchurch, a little further north. Here is the castle of the de Bolebecs, or at least earthworks where the castle once stood, for the decaying building was finally raised by Cromwell's troops in the Civil War. Whitchurch Manor was one of 147 manors given to Walter Giffard de Bolebec by William the Conqueror, in recognition of his contribution to the assessment of the Domesday survey. Clearly he could not use them all, and Whitchurch Manor was held for him by his relative Hugh, who probably built the castle. It was de Bolebec's son, also called Walter, who founded Notley Abbey, a little further along the river, as we shall later see.

Before we leave this stretch of the Thame, we should note that although environmentalists may have achieved one decisive victory, the developers have not yet finished with Aylesbury's section of the Thame floodplain. The latest proposed major development, recently commenced, stretches across much of the outer north to north-west area of the town. The Weedon Hill development occupies land from the Buckingham Road to Quarrendon SAM, bounded to the south by the Thame. Indeed, the enabling road works for the development extend to within yards of Holman's Bridge. As was the case with the design of Watermead, the floodplain will be protected by the creation of a new 'informal linear park',[34] whilst balancing ponds and other measures will be incorporated to ensure that the Thame and other local watercourses are not adversely affected. Similarly, Berryfields, a much larger site of 195 hectares, spreading westwards from Quarrendon SAM to the railway line running roughly north from Aylesbury to Banbury, and extending southwards to the River Thame, will require measures to accommodate potential floodwater. The floodplain of the river and two of its feeder streams, Marston Brook and Hardwick Brook, will be retained within a recreational area provisionally described as 'Valley Park'.[35]

Any concessions to conservation are noted and welcomed, but the fact remains that another swathe of countryside will disappear irrevocably, and another chapter in the history of our rural heritage will close. Grave concerns have been expressed over the future of the Quarrendon SAM: what is an historic treasure to one may be simply 'a series of hills, dips and stones'[36] to another having little serious regard to the fascinating heritage of our land. The management and security of the area in the context of the inevitable redevelopment is a real cause for concern, and even featured in a BBC local news bulletin.

The traveller and writer William Cobbett (1762-1835) came of country stock, and was himself a somewhat controversial character. In *Rural Rides*, written in 1829, he describes, in words that would strike a chord with many today, how, 'a friend had that morning taken him to view the beautiful Vale of Aylesbury, which he had never before seen; and the first thought that struck him on seeing the rich pasture was this, Good God! Is a country like this to be ruined by the folly of those who govern it'?[37] Having noted similar disquiet in our own times at these various urban intrusions into our rural landscape, we should perhaps move quickly on, leave the environmental and conservation debate to one side, and return to our journey, focussing on less controversial issues as we continue downstream.

two

Aylesbury to Chearsley

the Tame goeth by Ethorpe, the Winchingtons, Coddington, Chersleie …

The river that is now unequivocally the River Thame heads south-westwards as it leaves Aylesbury, passing under a bridge on the A41 Bicester Road. The bridge is today identified as 'Stone Bridge 1993', the present version having replaced a two-span reinforced concrete structure built in 1927 that had been found to be weak. Despite the somewhat evocative name, a legacy of former times, it is in reality a somewhat utilitarian concrete and brick structure, surely very different from the stone bridge of the sixteenth century mentioned by both Leland, who specifically names it, 'Stone Bridge, on Tame, betwixt Ailesbery and Querendon'[38] and Holinshed, who describes it, 'from the stone bridge, that is betweene Querendon and Ailsburie (after the course of the water)'.[39] As Leland specifically names this 'Stone Bridge', it calls into question what bridge he was referring to as 'Woman's Bridge' when he wrote:

> Or evar I pasyd into Aillesbyri, I rode over a little bridge of Stone caulid Woman's Bridge, undar the which passith a Brooke downe on the right hand as I rode; and from this Bridge to the Towne is a Causey of Stone. (This is, as farre as I can gather, Tame Water).[40]

The Aylesbury charter of 1554 referred to earlier mentions a bridge on the Bicester Road called Stanne or Gallows Bridge: presumably this is Leland's Stone Bridge. The charter also mentions a Wall Bridge towards Hartwell, and Walton Bridge, on the eastern side of Aylesbury, but no Woman's Bridge. The need for a causeway would certainly fit with our knowledge of the marshy area around Holman's Bridge. Perhaps there is no mystery and the name was simply a transcription or printing error, and Leland was indeed alluding to Holman's Bridge.

For interest, and to complete his description of rivers and bridges around Aylesbury, we should note that Leland also mentions another bridge:

> There rennithe a praty brooke undar a Wooden Bridge, almost at the very End of Aillesbyri Towne, by Southe. This water cummithe downe from East and rennithe by Weste into Tame, by the lefte ripe of it about a mile bynethe Aillesbyri, some what lower then Stone-bridge on Tame. I take the hedde of this broke to be toward Wyndover thrwgh-fayre 3 miles of the Southe.[41]

It is not entirely clear whether this wooden bridge is one of the other bridges mentioned in the Aylesbury Charter – Wall Bridge towards Hartwell would be south-west of the town, Walton Bridge would be east or at best south-east – or somewhere else. Of the two named structures, Leland's description perhaps favours Walton Bridge as being his wooden bridge, built over Bear Brook or one of its feeder streams.

There is less confusion regarding Stone Bridge, and shortly after the river passes under the bridge, it is crossed by overhead power lines, with their incessant, rather disturbing, crackly hum, in the vicinity of the route taken by the Romans along Akeman Street, linking Verulamium (St Albans) and Alcester. The river snakes its way for a few hundred yards along the fringe of a recreational area and then is crossed by a railway track, the Aylesbury to Banbury line, which is bridged over the river by means of a concrete span on grey brick supports. Housing continues not far to the left behind the recreational area, followed soon by headwalls and discharge from Aylesbury sewage works. The local water authority was fined heavily in 2002 for allowing untreated sewage effluent to discharge from here to the River Thame, killing an estimated 15,000 fish. There is an environmental gain from the works, however, for it is home, temporary or otherwise, to quite a number of species of birds, each finding some particular benefit from the various habitats offered by different stages of the sewage process. As the technology for sewage treatment has evolved over the last thirty years, so the list of resident or transient species of birds has changed. As well as the common 'garden' birds, yellow wagtail, meadow pipit, chiffchaff, black redstart, reed bunting, greenshank, green sandpiper, and various waterfowl, to name but some, have been seen regularly, visiting or nesting for a greater or lesser part of this period.

Almost immediately after the sewage works, the river is joined by Bear Brook, itself much prone to flooding from time to time, and like the Thame, something of a bugbear to the planners in spite of its normally modest proportions. Perhaps this is Leland's 'praty brooke'. In the development of Fairford Leys, a substantial housing area in the south-west of Aylesbury, major flood protection measures had to be incorporated, not least the re-profiling of three watercourses, including Bear Brook, and the provision of a new flood compensation area. The junction with Bear Brook is followed quickly by the arrival, on the opposite side of the river, of Marston Brook from the north. This is itself an accumulation of several streams arising north and south of Quainton, and near to Pitchcott.

Once boosted these additions to its flow, the Thame finds itself relatively free of urban intrusion and the developers' schemes and dreams, though for some time the 'ever present monolith that is County Hall'[42] encroaches upon the skyline at certain points. It is not the only modern intrusion into the landscape. The sturdy 320-feet tall telecoms tower, set high away to the left on the Chilterns near Stokenchurch, and the spindly television mast at low-lying Beckley ahead to the right, stand like distant sentinels over the river plain. The river, untroubled, twists its way through a mile or so of open pasture, often wet or flooded, territory ideally suited to substantial numbers of birds, especially those over-wintering from Eastern Europe and Scandinavia. Here, and along other stretches of the river, large flocks of lapwing and starling may be seen, together with the now ubiquitous gulls, and at times, redwing and fieldfare.

Shortly past the site of the medieval village of Eythrope (the hamlet name is Anglo-Saxon in origin, and means 'island farm', referring to an island in the River Thame that flows by the hamlet), where the river briefly separates into two channels, two large mounds can be seen to the left. These are natural outcrops of hard Purbeck rock, similar to that found at nearby Brill. The river itself runs mostly over heavy clay, but close by to the south at this point, the geological map is a mosaic of colour, representing a great diversity of rock types. Excavations in 1906 revealed evidence of ancient burials at the top of one of the mounds, Burn Hill, dating from Saxon or even Iron or Bronze Age times. Because much of the land around is relatively flat, good views along the Thame valley are commanded from the top of these curious tree-topped prominences.

The course of the river here is closely followed by the routes and intersections of a number of footpaths – the Aylesbury Ring, the North Bucks Way, the Midshires Way, and, of more immediate interest, the Thame Valley Walk, a fifteen-mile trail from Aylesbury to Albury, linking the North Bucks Way to the Oxfordshire Way, and following the general course of the Thame. The walk, formally launched in 1993, is rarely more than a field or so away from the river, but diverts occasionally to take in places of interest such as Long Crendon and Rycote chapel. It takes the rambler through the characteristic water meadows of the Thame valley, with its ubiquitous accompaniment of willows and the occasional black poplar, a tree we will look at in greater detail shortly. Crack willow, with its coarsely ridged and fissured bark, is present in profusion, and many willows have been pollarded, following in the ancient tradition of cutting off a maturing tree at a height of about eight feet or so, above the reach of grazing animals. Older pollards, often with huge, gnarled trunks, are a haven for wildlife: lichens grow on the bark, many insect species thrive on the mouldering crown and interiors, and birds and bats nest and roost within.

The Midshires Way is a long-distance footpath and bridleway that runs about 225 miles through the centre of England, linking the Icknield Way and the Ridgeway with the Trans-Pennine Trail, and then on to the Pennine Way. It starts its northwards journey south of the Thame at Bledlow, on the slopes of the Chilterns, and close to the source of Lyde Brook, one of the little streams that feed eventually into the River Thame. Bledlow's Holy Trinity church is perched, seemingly rather precariously, on the edge of a deep ravine, with Lyde Brook at the bottom, fed by numerous springs and rivulets, many of them arising in the rather chalky bank that supports the church. The intrinsic appeal of the ravine has been enhanced by its transformation into a water garden, complete with networks of paths, bridges and seats, an unexpected haven of tranquillity in already calm countryside, with little more than the sound of trickling and tumbling water to disturb the silence.

Eythrope Bridge.

The River Thame, meanwhile, divides again near Weir Lodge, at the lower eastern tip of Eythrope Estate. The lodge is one of a number of rather ornate rustic Victorian lodges on the estate, each one bearing the Five Arrows insignia of the Rothschilds. The arrows signify the five sons of Baron Mayer Amschel von Rothschild (1744-1812) who went out to found banks in the five principal financial centres of Europe in the nineteenth century, and the insignia is much in evidence in and around Waddesdon, home to members of the Rothschild family for well over 100 years.

Alice de Rothschild built Weir Lodge for the boatman employed to steer boats for family guests up the lake to another riverside lodge for afternoon tea. At the lower western end of the Eythrope Estate, Bridge Lodge, with its striking chimney stacks, lies near to a waterfall that is in turn next to a bridge on the site of a watermill that went out of use in the seventeenth century. In the 1880s, the mill site was dammed in order to raise the level of the millstream to form an ornamental lake along the southerly limit of the Estate, thereby enhancing the view from the house.

The bridge is a rather stumpy, stone-built structure with coarse rendering over some surfaces, and with stone-carved corbel-like heads set towards the apex on either side. The bridge's east facing side has been redressed but retains a perfunctory layer of presumably, original stone, including the corbel. There is no integral parapet or balustrade, though there are token metal and wood handrails clearly added at a much later date, and looking somewhat out of character with the rest of the structure. Nearby, a more modern bridge built of red brick crosses the River Thame, which at this point is narrower than its subsidiary millstream.

Eythrope Estate is an area of farm and wooded parkland where sheep and heron can graze and forage the same peaceful meadows with obvious mutual indifference, whilst buzzards glide and circle effortlessly in the skies above. The estate surrounds one of the great houses built across the Vale of Aylesbury in the nineteenth century by the Rothschild family. Previously it had been the site of a mansion owned successively since 1309 by the Arch, Denham, Dynham, Dormer and Stanhope families. A chapel had been built in 1490 by Sir Roger Dynham, only to be pulled down by one of the Stanhopes, Sir William, who, 'most wickedly, sacrilegiously and impiously demolished the chapel, though warned against it'.[43] In 1738 he made use of the stones to build the nearby bridge over the Thame millstream. Another of the Stanhopes pulled down the mansion house in 1812, also seemingly in a fit of pique over some local political rivalry.

The Rothschilds acquired the neighbouring Waddesdon estate from the Duke of Marlborough in 1874, and within about ten years had built a new house, Waddesdon Manor, that was later (in 1957) bequeathed to the National Trust. In 1883, another new house, a pale pink brick-and-stone 'Pavilion', complete with turrets and gables, was built on the Eythrope estate for Alice, the unmarried sister of Baron Ferdinand de Rothschild. Alice had purchased Eythrope in 1875 but continued to live for a while with her brother at Waddesdon. The Pavilion was built, not on the site of the previous manor, but in a field near the lake, the flooded arm of the Thame, and strange though it may seem to us, Alice occupied her new home only in the daytime, having been advised that to sleep near water would exacerbate the rheumatic fever from which she suffered. Indeed, the Pavilion was deliberately built without bedrooms so that she would not be tempted to stay overnight, and Alice always returned the four miles to Waddesdon Manor at night time when the damp air came off the river.

Following Alice's death in 1922, the Pavilion was let to a tenant, the widow of writer Somerset Maugham, who extended the property to include the missing bedrooms and bathroom. Alice, incidentally, was a close friend of Queen Victoria, who referred to her as 'She who must be obeyed'[44] following an incident at Alice's French Riviera home, when she rebuked the Queen for walking on some of her flowers. It was perhaps due more to Chiltern's author John Mortimer, writing for his popular television character *Rumpole of the Bailey* in the late 1970s, that the phrase came into common vernacular, albeit with a slightly different connotation.

As we have just passed the site of a former watermill, and rapidly approach two more, it is perhaps a suitable moment to comment briefly on one or two aspects of watermills, as they will continue to be an occasional, albeit historical, feature of our journey. Watermills were probably introduced into the British Isles by the Romans, and of the 9,250 manors mentioned at the time of the Domesday survey, 3,463 had between them 5,624 mills. Right up until the introduction of steam power during the Industrial Revolution, moving water continued to provide the main source of industrial energy in Britain, though windmills also became common after the second half of the twelfth century.

In medieval times watermills were used primarily for milling, drainage and fulling. A paddlewheel, usually of elm wood, turned in the water and drove the millstone via an axle and a system of interlocking cogwheels. Most Domesday mills were of the undershot type, whereby the wheel was turned by water running underneath the wheel to catch the blades. Later, the overshot type increased in popularity: water was carried over the top of the wheel and then dropped onto the blades to turn the wheel. The later system required less water but did require an adequate fall, usually accomplished by incorporating sluice gates, a weir or other similar device, and would often involve diversion of the main river through a subsidiary stream.

Most of the mills mentioned in the Domesday Book were corn mills, used for grinding grain into flour for bread, and many, being of wooden construction, would actually be burnt down, the friction caused by wooden machinery igniting explosive flour dust. As was the case with medieval bridges, also often built mostly of timber, and liable to be destroyed by surging flood waters, this was good news for the local carpenter, but not so for the owner and even less so for other users. Tenants of the manor were forced to use the mill attached to their manor and were obliged to pay both the miller and the lord for the privilege. Later, and until well into the eighteenth century, when technology improved, watermills were used to drive looms and saw mills. Not surprisingly, many local watermills are now little more than an historical fact. In some cases, there are remains, in a few cases whole buildings survive, but to be preserved in potential working order is something of a rarity, and sadly not a feature we will encounter on this particular journey.

We should make mention of the elm, referred to earlier in connection with its use as the preferred timber for the manufacture of paddlewheels. In fact, the elm was as much a symbol of the English countryside as was the oak, and has been intimately linked to many aspects of rural life for centuries. Everything changed when disease struck the elm for certainly the second time in recorded history. The first probable outbreak of disease is deduced from the substantial evidence of a massive decline in the elm population in the Neolithic period around 3700 BC. It is thought that at that time, around half the European population of elms was destroyed, though whether this was due exclusively to disease or some other cause remains unclear. Nearly 5,500 years later, disaster struck again. Any reader born before the late 1960s may well recall a devastation to the elm population, and with it the landscape generally, caused in the 1970s by Dutch elm disease. It is estimated that approximately 25 million trees were lost over the course of a decade or so. Buckinghamshire was one of the first, and worst, areas affected, and the Thame valley and countryside to either side was certainly not immune to the decimation. The landscape was changed, if not irrevocably, certainly for the lifetime of those who witnessed the calamity.

Dutch elm disease is one of the most serious arboreal diseases in the world, and the English elm (*Ulmus procera*) is particularly susceptible. The disease is caused by two related species of fungi of the genus *Ophiostoma* which are disseminated from tree to tree by elm-bark beetles of the genus *Scolytus scotylus*, which feed in the upper branches of the tree and introduce fungal spores to exposed tissue. The disease has no cure, and control methods involve injecting insecticide into the trees annually to prevent infection, or the destruction of all elms in a broad band around an infected area, to keep the beetles out. The loss of elm trees in our area of interest seems to have been almost 100 per cent, though there are some signs of a gradual recovery. Further cycles of the disease can be expected, but experts are confident the elm will survive to provide a potential contribution to future landscapes.

Like the elm, the black poplar (*Populus nigra subspecies betulifolia*) was for centuries central to rural life, being much used in mill buildings and for brake blocks, as it is heat and fire resistant. Its shock absorbent properties were exploited in wagon construction and it was used to make rifle butts in the First World War. Thin branches from pollarded black poplars were sometimes used for hurdles and fruit baskets in place of hazel or willow. The black poplar is now one of Britain's most rare native trees and is listed as an endangered species. It is characterised by a large, often leaning and ungainly appearance, with massively arching down-curved branches and heavily ridged trunk. It has separate male and female trees, with red ('Devil's fingers') and green catkins respectively, the latter producing copious amounts of fluffy seed. The male and female trees occur in a ratio of about fifty to one, so seedlings are rare and the poplar normally reproduces by rooting from fallen trees. It is a tree of wet woodland and forested wood plain. In Britain such habitats have steadily disappeared since Neolithic times through land drainage and woodland clearance, and black poplar are now only found in wet areas, typically alongside streams and rivers, particularly where these form floodplains and water meadows.

Some estimate that up to fifty per cent of Britain's population of black poplars is found in the Aylesbury area, not least along the banks of the Thame. Black poplars can live for over 250 years and there are historical records of individual trees dating back to before 1715. Virtually all mature black poplars remaining in Britain probably date from before 1850, as very few have been planted since that time, and the majority of surviving native black poplars are approaching the end of their natural life spans. We have finally woken up to this serious state, and concerted efforts are now being made locally at several points around Aylesbury, and on or near the Thame, to carry out major replenishment of this protected species.

As we continue on our way from Eythrope, the remains of a rectangular moat can be seen in the meadow close to the right hand bank of the Eythrope millstream and behind this a hill rises quite steeply. The stream rejoins the main river and there is evidence of old disused fishponds nearby, with their internal divisions to separate the breeding areas. We reach a point on the river where two villages occur in quick succession, one on either side of the river. Cuddington is set back some little way, but Nether (or Lower) Winchendon reaches close to the river, and perhaps not surprisingly, the first house we pass is built on the site of the former Nether Winchendon Mill. There was a mill here at the time of the Domesday survey, and later it produced paper as well as flour, though there is now little evidence of this

Nether Winchendon Mill, miller's house and mill race, photographed in 1939. (From the Buckinghamshire County Museum collections, by kind permission)

activity, and even the millstream has all but disappeared, choked by silt and a mass of reeds.

The name Winchendon is probably of Anglo-Saxon origin, meaning 'hill at a bend' or 'springs on a hillock'; in the Domesday Book it is called Wincandone. Some have suggested that the name Winchendon is derived from an old English name for a lapwing, a bird still to be seen in fields around the village. Nether Winchendon itself is a pretty village. At its centre is a small green on which stands a rather unusual Victorian letterbox set in a stone pillar with a ball on top. Nearby is the little church of St Nicholas, whose most immediately striking feature is a blue-and-gold-faced, single-handed clock, bequeathed to the church in 1722 by Jane Beresford of Nether Winchendon House. An inscription reminds all those who hear the clock to, 'spend their time in honest discharge of their calling and in the worship of God that repentance may not come too late.' The lengthy fourteen feet-long pendulum stretches towards the foot of the tower, and can be seen from within the church that has features enough of its own. It has a simple external structure with partly plastered stonewalls, a red-tiled roof and rather uneven tiled floor. Cobbles and rough-hewn stones at the base of the bell tower are possibly lingering traces of an earlier Saxon building. The bells themselves include one dated 1620, another dated 1631 and two dated 1640. The nave and chancel are fourteenth century; the font, some of the stained glass and two of the brasses are fifteenth century, as are some of the seats under the gallery which bears the royal coat of arms of George II, whilst the canopied, three-decker Jacobean pulpit, dated 1613, with its reading desk and clerk's stall, looks out over high-boxed pews from the eighteenth century. Elsewhere there is sixteenth-century Flemish glass and, unusually, perhaps, a mid-twentieth-century brass.

The village lays claim to a 'celebrity' of Tudor times. Lettice Knolleys, supposedly born in Winchendon, was a cousin to Queen Elizabeth I, and indeed as children, they were very close. In later life, however, Lettice was to become the object not only of gossip and scandal, (doubtless much to the disappointment of her Puritan statesman father, Sir Robert Knolleys), but also the wrath of her Queen. Lettice married the first Earl of Essex, but even before his rather premature death, she had seemingly embarked on a lengthy affair with Robert Dudley, who was Earl of Leicester, but more significantly, the Queen's favourite. Not surprisingly, Elizabeth was furious when she discovered that Lettice had subsequently married Dudley. He later died, like Essex, in rather dubious circumstances, and there was speculation that both husbands had been poisoned. Undaunted, Lettice married a third time, on this occasion to Sir Christopher Blount, a man young enough to be her son. This marriage too was fairly short-lived, as both Blount and Lettice's son by Essex, who in spite of the age difference had also become very close to Elizabeth, were executed in 1601 following an ill-fated attempt to overthrow the government. Lettice, meanwhile, lived on to the age of ninety-four, having lived through the reigns of seven English sovereigns. We mentioned earlier the claim that Lettice was born in Winchendon in 1540; some records indicate that her birthplace was actually at Rotherfield Grays near Henley. She became related in a rather roundabout way to Sir Antony Lee of Quarrendon, to whom we also referred earlier, when her widowed grandmother married Sir Antony's father, Sir Robert Lee of Burston.

Of the many timber-framed structures in Winchendon, the manor farmhouse, at one time the Knolleys' family home, is particularly imposing, standing on a slope to the west of the church. Much of the house pre-dates the door dated 1620. Clustered around St Nicholas' church are houses and cottages in a range of styles, with some properties dating back to the sixteenth and seventeenth centuries, perhaps the very same buildings that would have been familiar to Lettice, if our assumption concerning her birthplace is correct. Other cottages are conspicuous for the colour wash of ochre on their walls, in a russet tint that denotes ownership by the Spencer-Bernard family, owners of Nether Winchendon House.

Nether Winchendon House, or the Priory as it has been known, is of medieval origins. In the early eleventh century, the Manor was an estate of Queen Edyth, the wife of Edward the Confessor. After the Norman Conquest, it was acquired and later, possibly as early as 1216, given as a grange to the reformed Augustine monks at Notley Abbey by Walter Giffard, the Earl of Buckingham. After the dissolution of the Abbey in 1547, the Manor was granted to the 1st Earl of Bedford. In time the property passed by direct descent or marriage to the Bernard (later Spencer-Bernard) family, and Scrope Bernard was responsible for major gothicisation of the property in 1797-1803. His efforts were not entirely well received, for it is said that Scrope Bernard's wife so disliked the end result that the couple went to live in the rectory at Kimble. In our own day, one observer has described the house as possessing, 'a riot of spiral brick chimneys, castellations, bell tower and garrets on every conceivable corner'.[45]

Approached by a lane leading from the green, the house may be seen through a picturesque stone screen of three arches, built in the mid-eighteenth century. The view from the river, near an ornate bridge, is similarly striking. The bridge is the middle of three, crossing the river in the vicinity of Nether Winchendon. Soon after the third, which bears the date 1945 in a concrete insert within timber planks, the river divides yet again as it curves temporarily southward. Each branch passes under its own three-arched bridge on the Cuddington to Chearsley road (along a stretch known as Bridgeway); both bridges are built of grey brick, rather similar in style to Holman's Bridge, with both having two cut-waters. Both streams are crossed by a large ungainly pipe, and soon pass Cuddington Mill Farm, whereupon the two streams rejoin.

Cuddington Mill probably once belonged to Notley Abbey. It is mentioned in records from 1588, but not as far back as the Domesday Book in the eleventh century, when the nearby village was listed as 'Cudintuna'. The village now known as Cuddington (from an Anglo-Saxon name, meaning 'Cuda's estate') is in our time a small, well-kept neighbourhood, set back from the river on a slightly higher ridge top from where panoramic views over the flat water meadows of the Thame to Nether Winchendon can be enjoyed.

Cuddington, and indeed its mill, can lay claim to a link to Boddington's Brewery, producers of the 'Cream of Manchester'. Henry Boddington was employed as a traveller for Strangeways Brewery in Manchester, worked his way up through the company, and eventually, with son Henry Junior, renamed the brewery with the Boddington family name. Henry was born in Thame in 1813, but his father, John Boddington (1777-1839), was born at Cuddington Mill and became a miller himself, and John's father, grandfather and great-grandfather were all baptized and buried in the village.

Cuddington, which is regularly well-placed in 'Best Village' competitions and displays a tally of its successes on one of its little greens, is built around a network of interconnecting narrow lanes, many of which are lined with witchert walls, mostly topped with tiles. Witchert is a uniquely Buckinghamshire type of earth walling, and is a variant of the West Country 'cob' walling. The name 'witchert' (or wytchert) is derived from a local clay – 'white earth' – and examples are found in several of the villages on or near our journey along the Thame, most noticeably in Haddenham, just a few miles 'inland' from Cuddington.

As it is such a unique form of building, we should pause once again and consider the nature of this very Buckinghamshire tradition. The construction of witchert

Cuddington Mill, date unknown. (Photograph by kind permission of Derek and Jean McCullagh)

walls entails wetting of the subsoil, a chalky clay, mixing it with chopped up straw, and then building it up in two feet tall layers ('berries') on a base foundation of stone and rubble (the 'grumpling'), the whole often covered with white-washed rendering. Left to dry, the mix forms a brick-hard substance that, unlike wattle-and-daub or lathe-and-plaster, requires no support. Additionally, witchert is easily moulded in construction, giving rise to characteristically rounded walls with irregular corners. As well as free-standing walls, which would be topped off with thatch or terracotta tiles to prevent the witchert becoming wet, the technique was much used in the construction of houses and farm buildings, and is one of the many and picturesque styles of building evident in Cuddington.

By contrast, the church of St Nicholas is built of light grey local limestone, with dark red tiles, and has a tall, embattled west tower. Externally, it does have the look of a somewhat piecemeal construction about it, but like many local churches it offers an interesting blend of styles and features dating back to the thirteenth century. There has been a church on the site since the late eleventh century, but the present chancel dates from around 1220, with much of the remainder of the building having been constructed in four stages over the rest of the century, with the tower being added about 200 years later. The font, with its oak and iron-bound lid, dates from the thirteenth century, but many other fittings date from the mid-Victorian era when the whole church was extensively renovated and restored.

Not much further along the river, the village of Chearsley can be seen nestling on the hillside to the right. Two footbridges cross the river here, the second one immediately followed by another unsightly pipe encased in concrete blocks. The first bridge is a rather smart wooden affair, the second a newly refurbished structure with gated, galvanised iron railings and a tarmac surface, and for now looking conspicuously new alongside nearby gnarled and twisted pollarded willows that have a distinctly ancient look about them.

Chearsley is another attractive witchert village, though with fewer buildings constructed in this manner, the local public house being a prominent example. Nonetheless, Chearsley has a character of its own, with a tangle of narrow, sunken village roads, originally formed well before metalled roads made their impact. An earlier village, which lay between the church and the River Thame, dated from ancient times and probably grew up around a small collection of scattered farmsteads. Chearsley, meaning 'Cerded's clearing' may be the 'Cerdicesleah' mentioned in the Saxon Chronicle, where it is alleged King Cerdic and his son Cynric defeated the Britons in AD 527. It is said they had established the kingdom of Wessex after arriving in Britain in AD 495, and probably operated in the Thames valley area, based around Dorchester, the end point of our journey along the Thame.

The Black Death decimated the population of Chearsley in 1348, and when a new generation of workers returned to take advantage of fertile fields, they sensibly built the village rather higher up the hillside, away from the floodwaters of the river. Leland remarked that the fields around Chearsley were 'exceedingly fruitful, mellow and tender' and as a consequence were likely to be overstocked with cattle. He also warned that they could be 'flotten and utterly spoiled'[46] by the regular floods.

The flooding and fruitfulness, in part, go hand in hand. In the seventeenth and eighteenth centuries, surprisingly sophisticated methods were used to take advantage of the regular flooding of water meadows, and induced flooding became an accepted strategy. The technique was most popular in chalkland areas, as the spring and river waters were rich in dissolved minerals acquired as rainwater percolated through the chalk. As a consequence in our own case, the Thame's eutrophic waters support a wide variety of submerged, emergent and bank-side vegetation such as stonewort, water lily, marsh marigold, hemp agrimony and willow herb, not to mention willow and black poplar described previously, but also, and more significantly, deposit their supply of nutrients over the surrounding fields during flooding.

Originally, Chearsley was a hamlet in the parish of Long Crendon, but in 1458 it became a parish in its own right. The church of St Nicholas lies towards the bottom of the hill, close to the river meadows, with the remains of a sizeable moat not far away. Like its namesake at nearby Cuddington, the church is built of local light-grey limestone, with a red-tiled roof and stone walls, plastered internally, and similarly reveals features dating back to the eleventh century, and almost every century since. Perhaps the most striking feature to the casual visitor is the timbered ceiling, dating back some 600 years, and the massive royal arms of George II on the north wall

Constructing the railway viaduct near Chearsley, *c*. 1903. (From the Record Office for Leicestershire, Leicester and Rutland, by kind permission)

of the nave. The fluted-font bowl dates from Norman times and the walls still bear traces of medieval frescoes. Although it has evolved to be what it now is over the greater part of 1,000 years, it still has the superficial appearance and feeling of an old village church that has always been that way.

Not far from the church a spring arises, Stock Well or Cherdeley Well, its stream trickling down the short descent to the Thame river. Not much further down the river, Dadbrook joins from the left. It rises at 'The Strangewell', close to Dadbrook House on the fringes of Cuddington, and in times past was believed to have curative medicinal qualities.

A little further along we reach the point where the Marylebone to Birmingham railway line is carried over the river, by means of the second of the two railway bridges over the Thame that are still functional. Built in the early 1900s, it is a sturdy, five-arched, mostly brick viaduct, constructed originally for the Great Western and Great Central Joint Line. The line, which first operated in 1910, was the last major railway engineering project to be undertaken in England until the Channel Tunnel was built some seventy-five years later, in 1986. There are regular protrusions from the parapet, these being recesses for gangers and platelayers to allow them to step clear of the tracks as trains approached.

Our next landmark requires that we step back further in time again, more than six centuries in fact, well before the era of George Stephenson, Richard Trevithick or Isambard Kingdom Brunel and the network of tracks and bridges spawned by their inventive endeavour and engineering skill.

three

Notley to Thame

> by ... Notleie abbeie: and comming almost to Tame ...

Around the year 1160, Walter Giffard, Earl of Buckingham, with his wife Ermengarde, established in their park at Crendon a home for a group of reformed Augustine (Arrouaisian) monks. These men filled a role partway between that of traditional monks and of secular clergy. They had a reputation for following a strict, some would say severe code of living, including silence, except during worship, and were known as 'black canons' because of their dress of black cloaks and hoods worn over white tunics. Giffard called the place Noctele, Nutley, or *de Parco* Crendon. Now known as Notley Abbey, and sited close to the banks of the Thame, it was to become for a time one of the largest and wealthiest Augustine monasteries in the region, though it has not subsequently enjoyed the lasting historical fame of others such as Dorchester or St Frideswide's. It was certainly prestigious in its day, however, and as well as its regular functions it served as a suitable place of correction for monks from other establishments who had strayed or become corrupt.

As was often the case in medieval times, the building of the church alone took a long time, in this case about 100 years. Extensions to the church and completion of other buildings including the Abbot's house continued, in fact, until about ten years before the dissolution of the monasteries by Henry VIII. At the time of the Dissolution, former monastic lands and buildings were systematically seized and sold or given to favoured courtiers, largely creating the economic power-base of the gentry and nobility that remains to this day. Henry VIII, who was a passionate supporter of learning, had stayed at Notley on several occasions when travelling to Oxford and its University with Cardinal Thomas Wolsey, but later showed scant regard for the monks' earlier hospitality (or indeed, for Wolsey's loyal service); at the Dissolution, the monks were evicted from the Abbey, much of which was destroyed in 1538, surviving structures being used later as a farm. Wolsey died a broken man, out of favour with the King, and with an accusation of treason over his head.

The present buildings at Notley, dating from the fifteenth and sixteenth centuries, incorporate some components, such as arcading and doorways, from the original structure, the greater part of the present house being derived from the Abbot's lodging. It has remained a prestigious dwelling: stars of stage and screen Laurence Olivier and his wife Vivien Leigh lived here between 1944 and 1959 for the greater part of their tempestuous twenty-year marriage.

Notley Mill in 1904.

The abbey took its name from the nut trees that in medieval times grew in abundance in the surrounding woods. Presumably with this in mind, Sir Laurence had the notion, in homage to his beautiful wife, star of the classic 1939 film *Gone with the Wind*, to plant a romantic nut walk beside the formal lawns that slope gently down from the house to the banks of the Thame. Vivien Leigh in turn planted a double arcade of lime trees along the half-mile drive from the main Thame-Aylesbury road to the house; years later she was said to be devastated when her beloved sixty-nine-acre home had to be sold due to her impending divorce from Olivier.

Two arches over the river and stream and some pieces of brickwork around the millraces are the only remaining signs of a succession of watermills that had existed on the site for centuries, the last one not being demolished until well into the twentieth century.

Nearby, a dovecote remains as a fine example of the thousands that were built from the time of the Norman Conquest onwards when pigeons were bred chiefly for food, though also for their manure, and in later centuries for saltpetre – a component of dung that was used to make gunpowder. In the earlier days, the right to build a dovecote was enjoyed by barons, abbots, lords of the manor, and parish priests, and this feudal privilege lasted well into the seventeenth century. From this time onwards, as restrictions were lifted, large numbers of dovecotes were built by a new generation of more prosperous freeholders and tenant farmers alike. Many of them seized the opportunity to share in the status accorded to this time-honoured privilege by building quite elaborate and ornamented structures. The later decline of the dovecote has been linked with the eighteenth-century introduction of the turnip, which enabled more animals to be kept over winter for a supply of fresh meat.

The Notley dovecote, on a hill overlooking the remains of the abbey and the river below, is a good-sized, square, stone building, with a tiled hipped roof, that probably dates from the Middle Ages, though estimates range from the fourteenth to seventeenth centuries. Certainly it is more likely that it pre-dates the Oppression of the late fifteen thirties. Its most striking feature, seemingly fairly unique among dovecotes, concerns the interior design: projecting inwards from the walls of the dovecote are shorter walls, all fitted with nest-holes, allowing provision for an estimated 4-5,000 pairs of birds. A prototype medieval battery farm, making efficient use of space, maybe, but hardly pleasant living conditions for the birds.

No such problem in our own time for the red kite, one of Britain's finest birds, now commonly to be seen soaring majestically above the Thame valley, as often over urban as over rural locations. Because it has become such an iconic figure in the area, we should perhaps pause again, and look at a little of the background of this splendid creature.

With its distinctive forked tail, russet plumage and massive five to six feet wingspan, the red kite was once common over the whole country, but had all but disappeared in Britain by the twentieth century. In its former heyday, the kite was well documented in British literature, the latter recording both the character and human perceptions of this magnificent bird. For example, Chaucer, *c.* 1343-1400, made reference to it in his *Knight's Tale*:

We stryve as did the houndes for the boon,
They foughte al day, and yet hir part was noon;
There cam a kyte, whyl that they were wrothe,
And bar away the boon betwixe them bothe.[47]

The kite was often to be seen over London, meriting regular mention from Shakespeare (1564-1616), who, according to some commentators, was describing his capital when he wrote of 'a city of kites and crows'.[48] Later, in *The History of England Book IV* (1670), John Milton (1608-1674) referred to the same pairing in the course of his comments concerning early English history, 'Such bickerings to recount, met often in these our writers, what more worth is it than to chronicle the wars of kites or crows flocking and fighting in the air'.[49]

Kites were unpopular on two counts. Firstly, in spring, nest-building kites were likely to snatch soft clothing for nest-lining material. Not surprisingly, washerwomen were somewhat irritated by the need to guard their laundry, left to dry on lines or hedges. Shakespeare made reference to this curious form of larceny in *The Winter's Tale*, when the street-wise Autolycus says, 'My traffic is sheets; when the kite builds, look to lesser linen'.[50]

Secondly, and perhaps more importantly, kites were erroneously perceived to be a threat to game birds, lambs and other livestock, though in reality, carrion forms the major component of their diet. Largely as a result of this misperception, and linked to the increasing availability of firearms, the kite underwent a cruel and relentless persecution between the seventeenth and nineteenth centuries to the point of virtual extinction, with just a few pairs remaining in mid-Wales.

The kite is mentioned in ancient biblical texts (eg Leviticus 11 v. 14), but our present-day name for the kite, which lends its name to the children's toy, is derived from the Anglo-Saxon word *cyta*, probably meaning 'to swoop swiftly'. In the past, it has been known by other names, the most widespread, and sharing similar derivation to the word for 'glide', being gled, glede or glead. The Hebrew word translated as 'glede' in the *King James Old Testament* (Deuteronomy 14 v. 13) is rendered as 'red kite' in more modern translations. *Gled* is the Gaelic for kite or hawk, and even some old place names, such as Gledsmuir, in the Scottish Borders, take their name from the same word. In his version of the old song *Killiecrankie,* Robert Burns (1759-1796) used the name gled when referring to the kite's habit of feeding on carrion, even of the human kind:

The bauld Pitcur fell in a furr,
And Clavers gat a clankie, O,
Or I had fed an Athole gled,
On the braes o Killiecrankie, O! [51]

In his poem *September*, John Clare (1793-1864), adjudged by some to be the greatest nature poet, likewise referred to the harsh reality of the nature of the bird:

The circling kite that round them flyes
Waiting the chance to seize the prize. [52]

Later, though writing in a different era and a different context, Rudyard Kipling (1865-1936) similarly alluded to the kite's grisly predilection for human carrion in his war poem, *Oonts:*

It ain't no jam for Tommy, but its kites an' crows for 'im. [53]

An alternative name for the kite, sometimes used by Shakespeare, is the puttock or paddock and in a poem entitled *The Fens*, John Clare also used this version in his evocative description of the kite in flight:

Ah, could I see a spinney nigh,
A paddock riding in the sky,
Above the oaks, in easy sail,
On stilly wings and forked tail. [54]

The kite was reintroduced to the Chilterns in a project running from 1989-1994, and now there are more than 130 pairs of these magnificent creatures gracing the Thame valley, seemingly in an ever-widening area, even reaching, once again, the skies above London. The resurgence is not limited to our area, however, there being a reported 700 pairs nationwide, some of these having been 'relocated' to other parts of the country from the Chilterns.

Whether wheeling effortlessly on a thermal, high in the sky, or engaging in aerial combat with Milton's over-attentive crows, when a shrill, quavering 'weeeeeeoo-weoo-weoo' often draws attention to its presence, the kite is sometimes confused at a glance with the buzzard, another bird making something of a comeback in the area. Unlike the kite, the buzzard's recovery seems to be occurring without planned human intervention. Even though red kites are a protected species, their safety is still somewhat under threat. They are scavengers, as we have noted, feeding on the carcases of mammals and birds, and this makes them particularly vulnerable to being poisoned by meat bait laced with poison, whether or not they are the intended target. The highest fine ever in the UK for a poisoning offence involving birds was imposed by Thame Magistrates in 1997 following the deaths of three red kites – all killed by an insecticide used in this way. More recently, in 2003, the discovery of two red kites on the banks of the River Thame near Cuddesdon Mill led to an investigation that revealed the illegal use of the same insecticide.

Cuddesdon Mill is still some miles away. For now, we resume our journey and continue past the site of Notley Mill as the river pursues its gentle meandering course towards ancient Dorchester and 'Old Father Thames'. After a further division and rejoining of the river, a weir and a footbridge, the Thame soon passes two signs of more contemporary times.

First is an industrial estate, accessed by road from the bottom of the hill leading from Thame up to Long Crendon. A commercial venture here began shortly before the Second World War when a local man set up a small business, digging, grading, and selling gravel from the low-lying fields close to the River Thame. His endeavours led on to the formation of a nationally known company specialising in pre-cast concrete structures and now a fifty-acre industrial estate is to be found on the flat meadowland site beside the river, looking somewhat out of place in its otherwise pastoral surroundings.

A little further on and the river marks the lower boundary of the second evidence of our modern way of life, a golf practice range, a resource to satisfy the seemingly insatiable contemporary demand for ever more golfing facilities. For most of its existence thus far, the River Thame, like some of its precursors, has marked a series of parish boundaries. At this point, it assumes a greater significance as for some miles it also delineates the county boundary for Buckinghamshire and Oxfordshire. A few miles further on, when the river turns south near Waterperry, it ends its association with Buckinghamshire, the county that has given it birth.

As the river nears Thame, there follow four bridges in quick succession, three of them relatively new and, it has to be said, rather uninteresting, but necessary to

Flooding at site of service area, Thame, 1989. (Photograph courtesy of *The Thame Gazette*)

accommodate the twists of the river when in 1980 the Thame bypass was constructed and the Thame to Long Crendon road re-routed. The first of the four, Thamemead Bridge, carries the new stretch of the latter road, and is close to a petrol station and motel, built shortly after the road, on land that was previously a prime site for regular flooding. Indeed, the meadows the other side of this road and either side of the adjacent north-west bypass still do flood in quite dramatic fashion.

Shortly before the river disappears momentarily under Thamemead Bridge, it is joined by Scotsgrove Brook. For over 900 years, the water running through this little feeder stream of the Thame has powered a succession of watermills at Scotsgrove, grinding corn mostly for the villagers of nearby Haddenham. The mill actually remained a commercial entity until 1967, at which point a facility that had existed certainly since Domesday times came to an end.

There is invariably a public footpath or bridle path close to any watermill; this is not coincidence, but a throwback to the days when this was necessary to enable local villagers to bring their corn to the mill for grinding. Nowadays, of course, such activity is redundant as far as the vast majority of these little mills are concerned, and the footpaths have a largely recreational function. For mill owners in the modern era, it must undoubtedly be irksome to have a procession of walkers strolling through their property, particularly as the footpaths invariably pass so close to what are now private houses. Scotsgrove Mill came very much into prominence in 1972 when its new owner attempted to change the course of the footpath that runs by the mill. A rather acrimonious legal dispute followed, but the attempt to redirect the path failed, after a successful campaign opposing the proposed diversion by the people of Haddenham and the surrounding area. Fortunately, other mill owners in the area adopt a more pragmatic view, accepting that any inconvenience goes with the territory and is an inherent fact of country heritage and tradition.

Judging by its name, the little hamlet of Scotsgrove was presumably situated at or near a toll point. A little higher up the hill, the Thame to Aylesbury road forks, the right-hand road heading towards Haddenham; near this point there are commanding views of a broad stretch of the Thame valley. In wintertime, when the trees have shed their foliage, and the floods are at their peak, the panorama can be particularly spectacular. At other times, the patchwork of fields can be observed changing character with the seasons, the enduring cycle of the countryside: the lush green grass of spring; the bright mustard-yellow of oilseed rape in early summer; the delicate blue haze of an expanse of cultivated flax; the golden fields of wheat, perhaps initially streaked with crimson poppies, ripening to harvest; the gleaming, rich brown furrows of freshly tilled soil; the dense, pervasive, ground-clinging mists of autumn. Other changing images do not share a cyclical pattern: sheaves of corn have irrevocably given way to bales, and these in turn have now been complemented, if not superseded, by large bales and round bales – practical, maybe, but surely lacking the evocative charm of the traditional Constable landscape.

It is said that somewhere near here, a man was hanged. He was allegedly the last man to be hanged for stealing sheep, though whether 'last' is a local, county, or national milestone in social history seems rather less certain. We can be sure that the Thame bypass was not in his sights as he swung, nor were the second (Rycotewood Bridge) and fourth of our bridges (Cuttle Bridge), built in 1980 to carry the bypass towards a roundabout link to the A418 Oxford road.

Thame has long been at the heart of a network of roads, the most important in olden times being the ancient highway from Aylesbury to Tetsworth. Interestingly, most traffic to and from Oxford used this route, as the present Thame to Oxford road did not become a popular highway until well into the nineteenth century. Did William Shakespeare pass this way 200 or so years before? He would have travelled between Stratford-upon-Avon and the Globe Theatre in London on a number of occasions and 'Shakespeare's Way' is now a 146-mile long recognised walk along roads, bridleways and footpaths, devised to follow the shortest practical route between the two locations. Shakespeare regularly stayed at the Crown Inn in Oxford where he was on good terms with the landlord, and evidently even better terms with the landlord's wife, Jane Davenant, who some believe to be the 'Dark Lady' of *The Sonnets*. (Shakespeare is widely held to be the father of Jane's son, the writer William Davenant.) From Oxford, Shakespeare most likely travelled along at least some of the Thame valley, perhaps, as legend has it, staying in Thame itself, before crossing the leafy Chilterns and on into west London.

The town has another Shakespearean connection, by way of an event that showed that even mild Thame is able to stage its own real-life drama. In June 1587, The

Queen's Men, a group of players originally put together by the spymaster Francis Walsingham as a front for a roving propaganda machine, but gradually enjoying crowd-pulling popularity in their own right as a troupe of touring actors, were due to perform in Thame on their way to Stratford-upon-Avon. It was the time of the annual sheep clip, when the town's population increased considerably, not least because of the actors and musicians who gathered to entertain the farmers, buyers and tradesmen. Among the group were James Burbage, later the first theatrical entrepreneur in London and highly influential in Shakespeare's career, and William Knell, one of the leading young actors in the group. The hot-headed Knell became embroiled in an argument in the town with John Towne, a fellow-actor from the group, and in the ensuing struggle close to the White Hound Inn in the High Street, Knell was stabbed and killed by Towne, who drew his own sword in self-defence. 'That Shakespeare may have filled the vacancy [caused by Knell's death] is an intriguing speculation'.[55] Was this event the catalyst that within a year or so first prompted the country's greatest playwright to put pen to paper?

Shakespeare, both the man and his works, has come under close scrutiny from academics and historians alike in our own time, and there is no shortage of denigrators; perhaps Shakespeare's own words, uttered in *King Richard II* by Thomas Mowbray, the Duke of Norfolk, were something of a self-fulfilling prophecy, when he declared that, without spotless reputation, 'Men are but gilded loam, or painted clay'.[56]

Thame is built on a sandstone island and surrounded by clay through which run the River Thame and several tributaries that together almost encircle the town. Camden, in his topographical work *Britannia*, describes Thame thus: 'a mercate [market] town situate very pleasantly among rivers. For Thame passeth hard by the north side, and two rivers shedding themselves into it compass the same, the one on the east, the other on the west'.[57]

Based in Westminster where he had his 'day job', Camden spent most of his spare time travelling around the country collecting material for his massive work, and clearly speaks from personal knowledge as he authoritatively describes Thame and its waterways.

One of these, Cuttle Brook, itself an amalgamation of several lesser streams, follows a route even more tortuous than that of the Thame. It finally joins the river from the south shortly up-stream of the aptly named Cuttle Bridge on the north-western section of the bypass. Before this junction, and as it flows north past the western side of the town, Cuttle Brook meanders through an area that for centuries was used for grazing but that recently has been developed as a designated Local Nature Reserve. Even Cuttle Brook has risen sufficiently high from time to time to flood the Oxford Road at the point where it dips down to cross the brook before climbing again towards Priestend. It is alleged that in 1879, the brook gathered so much water as the result of a thunderstorm that it temporarily reversed the current of the River Thame and so drove back the water flowing under Crendon Bridge!

Crendon Bridge, date unknown.

This, the third of our quartet of bridges, known formally as Thame Bridge but often referred to locally as Crendon Bridge, spans the river in the area known by its Saxon name, Crendon Pills. It is situated not far past St Mary's church along the original Long Crendon road, a stretch of effectively redundant highway that now terminates just short of the bypass and that is gated at either end. It is the bridge, or at least the site of the bridge, by which Leland crossed the Thame, 'a little NNW from Tame church over Carenton bridge, of four stone arches'.[58] It actually comprises three bridges in one: that nearest the town crosses the river; the other two are built over small ponds, the Crendon Pills. In its heyday, the present bridge was a decent structure with stone pillars, iron railings and the sort of timber handrail that one could imagine around the decks of the *Titanic* or some similar luxury liner. A small plate attached to the railings briefly acknowledges that the river marks the county boundary.

There has been a bridge here since as far back as at least 1294 when records reveal that the bridge was broken up in the course of a dispute over the Prebend. In 1309, the then Bishop of Lincoln, John d'Alderby, granted funds to repair the bridge, but in 1335 it collapsed, and for quite a while there was argument as to who took responsibility for maintenance. Much later, in 1798, the 'most rampageous flood ever known'[59] swept a wagon off the causeway into the meadow below, though worse still, a boy drowned at Cuddington Bridge around the same time. In another flood in 1894, three of the arches of the bridge were completely washed away, necessitating a rebuilding of the bridge two years later for the sum of £4,600. To facilitate the work, a temporary roadway and plank bridge was erected over the meadows on the east side. Nowadays, the bridge, and indeed the road itself, are sadly neglected and seem bereft of the charm they once had.

It is not far from here, at Jemmett's Hole, away from the road in the Shabbington direction, that the so-called 'Thame Hoard' was found. In 1940, a local man out walking with his wife and dog, discovered a small collection of ten coins and five rings by the banks of the river, close to where some dredging had taken place a few months before. Now in the Ashmolean Museum in Oxford, the items date back to the fourteenth, fifteenth and sixteenth centuries, with the rings, both secular and ecclesiastical, being particularly valuable. Experts suggest the hoard belonged to the last Cistercian Abbot of Thame, and may have been stolen or hidden to prevent confiscation by the Crown at the time of the Dissolution.

The western side of the roadway at Crendon Bridge and south of the river downstream is land belonging to the Prebendal, built in 1146 by Bishop Alexander of Lincoln. At the peak of its ecclesiastical significance, the complex consisted of a hall, solar (usually, but not invariably, an upper room in a medieval hall normally reserved for the private use of the family), and chapel. In 1547, the year King Henry VIII died, the last Prebendary of Thame sold the property, on behalf of the then Bishop, Henry Holbeach, into the private ownership of Sir John Thynne, and by this transaction ended some 500-years association with Lincoln. The property gradually fell into disrepair and was used as a farmhouse and outbuildings, but was restored in 1836 when a wealthy local man converted the hall into a private residence.

Originally, three sides of the Prebendal grounds were bounded by moats, though these have subsequently been filled in, whilst the river formed a natural boundary on the northern side. A little further downstream, the river similarly is the boundary of another establishment, though one of a rather contrasting nature.

Parish workhouses existed in Thame as far back as 1777, but in 1836, a new Thame workhouse was built under the aegis of Thame Poor Law Union on a site between the River Thame and the Oxford Road in Priestend. It was designed to accommodate about 350 people, both men, women and children, and though living conditions were somewhat Spartan, not least in the food department, there was at least some attempt at Christmas to vary the otherwise monotonous dietary regime. The local press were in the habit of reporting the occasion, and in 1879, for example, recorded that:

> the whole of the inmates of the Thame Union Workhouse, on Christmas Day, were (through the liberality of the Guardians), regaled with a substantial dinner of old English fare – roast beef and plum pudding, with the usual accompaniments, supplemented by a supply of good ale, which was thoroughly enjoyed by all.[60]

This was followed by various other treats, including, on Boxing Day, a decorated Christmas tree.

Another fifty or so Christmases were to elapse before the workhouse closed in the early 1930s and before long, in 1935, Rycotewood College was founded on the site as an educational establishment, initially for young men from disadvantaged homes in the north-east of England. They were instructed in a range of rural skills, agricultural engineering and similar disciplines. In the late 1950s, the college was handed over to Oxfordshire County Council to run as a residential college, still specialising in agricultural engineering and related skills, but over ensuing years, it also established a fine national reputation for the teaching of furniture and cabinet making and restoration. Co-operation with other establishments of further education followed, and in 2003, Rycotewood College formally merged with two others to form the Oxford and Cherwell Valley College. At this point, the name 'Rycotewood College' formally disappeared, and within about two years, following a review of organisational structures and premises, so did the students. The buildings remain empty, while councils and developers debate the immediate fate of the site; the likely option at the time of writing is conversion of the listed building to flats, with concurrent construction of new houses on the surrounding land. For now, at least, two red-brick pepper-pot gatehouses stand forlornly either side of the locked and disused entrance gates, their future equally uncertain.

The association of Thame and Lincoln mentioned earlier dates back at least to the time of the Norman Conquest, but the settlement at Thame goes back much further than the Middle Ages. Archaeological evidence is scant, but there have been chance finds of flint implements (in Conduit Field in 1851 and Cuttle Brook in 1860), some Neolithic or Bronze Age pottery, some Iron-Age and Roman coins (a gold coin of Honorius [AD 395] found in the High Street in 1829, a gold coin of Cunobelin [King of the Catuvellauni circa AD 10-42] ploughed up at Priest End in 1843, and a coin of Julius Caesar [circa 100-44 BC] found in the Recreation Ground in the 1870s), and some Roman pottery (a cinerary urn found at Lashlake). It is likely that when the Romans first came to this part of the country, the Thame district, with the river playing a key role, formed the frontier between ancient warring factions – the Dobuni from the upper Thames Valley and Cotswolds area (Oxfordshire and Gloucestershire) and the Catuvellauni from the Chilterns (Buckinghamshire, Bedfordshire and Hertfordshire), for example, not to mention the Atrebati from the middle Thames Valley and south (Berkshire, Hampshire and Sussex). In later years, as we shall see, the Thame again was a crucial military boundary.

Doubtless a settlement grew up at Thame because the river could be forded here, and 'Old Thame' developed around the church, just to the south of the river, on land that was slightly higher than the floodplain of the river and Cuttle Brook, an area now known as Priestend. There are occasional glimpses of Thame in records from early times. Around AD 670, while he was resident in Thame, Wulfhere, King of Mercia, ratified a charter endowing a minster at Chertsey. In so doing, he confirmed Thame's status as an established Christian town. Wulfhere, son of Penda and related to the later famous King Offa, had been the first of the royal line to convert to Christianity. Later, the Anglo-Saxon Chronicle records that Oskytel, Archbishop of York and Suffragen Bishop of Dorchester, died in Thame on All Saints' Day, AD 971, having been resident in the town, perhaps at Thame Park, for some little while. His presence in the town is a further indication of the town's standing as an ecclesiastical centre in those distant times.

The Domesday Book indicates that the Manor of Thame belonged to Remigius de Fécamp, then Bishop of Lincoln, though prior to the Conquest, Thame belonged to the Bishop of Dorchester. Remigius was a Benedictine monk from coastal Normandy who had practically assisted William the Conqueror's cause, and was rewarded for his efforts and loyalty with the first available Bishopric in England.

According to some accounts, Thame has held a weekly market every Tuesday from 1183 when Walter de Coutances, Bishop of Lincoln, secured market charters for the town from Henry II. Possession of the local manors reverted to the King when the See of Lincoln briefly lay vacant from the latter part of the same century, but in 1215, King John restored the market charter to Bishop Hugh Trotman of Lincoln, (or Hugh de Welles, as he was sometimes known). Henry III later ratified this in 1227, and the market place still follows the typical boat-shaped appearance of a planted town, with relatively narrow entrances at either end. The market was originally held in the Buttermarket, by tradition on the cooler northern side, and the Cornmarket area on the southern side, with Middle Row, an area for temporary stalls, separating the two.

Around the same time, more than fifty acres of arable land were taken from the demesne and divided into burgage plots, each one having a house or shop with a long, narrow one-acre strip of land to the rear. The basic medieval layout in the centre of the town is still apparent today. The burgages, nominally rectangular, actually followed the curve formed by generations of plough teams turning at the end of the strip. This is evident even today on the north side of the Buttermarket, where passageways come out into the street. Back in 1230 there were sixty-three such plots, and by the fourteenth century, the number had risen to seventy-six, each one let at a minimal rent. Tenants had complete security of tenure, could sell or will their strips as they pleased, and later were allowed to divide the strips into half or quarter burgages. This whole approach was quite innovative for its time and proved to be a marked success that, like the market, attracted traders and craftsmen to the town.

Meanwhile, in 1219, Bishop Hugh Trotman of Lincoln made a very shrewd move when he applied for a licence to divert the Oxford to Aylesbury road through the town, charging travellers a toll for the privilege, but more importantly, bringing traders into the town. The economic boom enjoyed as a result of all these measures was enhanced by a reputation for fair-trading, upheld by a regular fortnightly court known as the Portmoot. The market prospered further when Bishop John d'Alderby managed to persuade King Edward I to withdraw the market charter from nearby Haddenham, on competitive grounds. Later, in 1657, the town lodged a successful petition against the establishment of a market in Aylesbury, and in 1683 it was declared that the market at Thame made the horse market in Oxford redundant. Like its market, the town flourished and 'New Thame' was born. As the town bears the name of the river we are exploring, perhaps it is not unreasonable to linger a while and look a little more closely at the town and some of its people.

four

Thame

> Tame standeth inuironed vpon thrée sides with thrée seuerall waters, as maie be easilie séene …

In the previous chapter we briefly traced the origins of the town of Thame, and saw how Old Thame gave way to New Thame as the heart of the community. We mentioned that Middle Row, which separated the two areas of the Thame market, originally consisted of stalls that were put up and taken down each week. Over the course of time, these temporary booths were gradually replaced by permanent structures, one of these being the Birdcage Inn, though in those early days it was known simply as 'the Cage'. Dating back at least as far as 1430, this half-timbered building, with its overhanging storeys and heavy gabled, almost fairy-tale like appearance, has a history of its own, not least as a holding place for several rather different categories of inmates. What is rather uncertain is the date of origin of its presumed early medieval stone-vaulted cellar, and particularly the arch therein, akin to that usually found in a church. The cellar probably remains from an earlier building that possibly, given its central location, may have had some administrative function within the market, and it is likely it was also used to hold prisoners in financial debt to the Bishop of Lincoln.

The Birdcage is known to have been used at one stage to house people with leprosy – they were isolated in one of the upper rooms and fed through a trapdoor by nuns. It may come as something of a surprise to some readers to find that there was a need for such accommodation in England, even in medieval times. Some diseases summarily described as 'leprosy' in those distant times would doubtless now be diagnosed rather differently, but true leprosy was endemic in England and gave rise to dedicated cemeteries and around 200 hospices, the so called lazar houses. The latter were particularly common in the Thames Valley and East Anglia, and information on bed-state versus population suggests an incidence of leprosy in the general population of at least one per cent. Those suffering from this debilitating disease were forced to wear a distinctive style of clothing comprising a mantle and beaver-skin hat, or a green gown. They would carry a bell or clapper, by which they could give warning of their approach so that everyone could get out of the way in time. Such was the stigma attached to the disease that one sufferer who had lived in the Birdcage was allegedly stoned to death by local town's people of Thame.

It is commonly supposed that warriors returning from the Crusades brought leprosy into the country, but there is evidence that it already existed in Britain before the first Crusade left in 1095. We cannot be sure why it disappeared as an endemic disease over succeeding centuries, to be virtually eradicated by the mid-sixteenth century. A number of factors have been suggested: effective isolation of sufferers; the Black Death in 1348–50, that killed off large numbers of the poorer levels of society where leprosy was most common; a mean average climatic temperature drop of two degrees Centigrade in the thirteenth century, such that the environment may have been less favourable to the causative bacteria; a gradually improving diet that may have predisposed to improved inherited resistance to the disease.

As the disease declined, so did the need for isolation facilities, such that by the time of the Napoleonic Wars, the Birdcage was available again for another group of detainees. In 1806, 100 or so French prisoners of war were held in Thame, the lower ranks housed in a cellar of the Birdcage Inn, while their officers were entertained in the Spread Eagle hotel opposite, though at this stage the property was probably still a private mansion house. In reality, their confinement was a fairly relaxed arrangement, for the prisoners were allowed the freedom of the town during the day, and some eventually took up residence and married local women.

The Birdcage remains in the town centre to the present day, recently refurbished but externally at least, losing nothing of its medieval appeal. Any visitor walking from there towards Priestend cannot fail to notice the increasing number of timber-framed buildings in the proximity of the church. Some are delightful and sufficiently picturesque to be included on calendars or chocolate boxes, though none seem to date much before the fifteenth century. Close to the church are the mid-fifteenth-century almshouses, founded by Richard Quartermain of North Weston Manor, a major benefactor of Thame and one-time 'minder' of Elizabeth I at Rycote. The jettied building, with its overhanging upper storey, was once home to seven of the town's poorest, six men and one woman. The cost of housing, feeding and clothing them came from the annual income gained from the rent of various pieces of land in the locality. The almshouses were suppressed at the time of the Reformation, but were subsequently refounded by Lord Williams, according to a bequest in his will, and used as such until the 1870s.

Even closer to the church is the attractive sixteenth-century timber-and-brick tithe barn. The medieval church was meticulous in exacting in kind its tithe of one tenth of the produce of its parish lands, and in some areas such tithes continued to be collected in this way until the early nineteenth century. It has become popular in our own times for these old barns to be converted to 'banqueting halls', one such locally being at Notley. Undoubtedly they have character and perhaps a certain romantic appeal, though some such transformations are more suited to their new purpose than others.

Thame's Lower High Street is a mix of buildings, some originating from the time of the burgages, others from Tudor, Stuart and Georgian periods. Facing up the street at Priestend, and built on land that adjoins that of the Prebendal, is the striking seventeenth-century house 'Stribblehills'. Of medieval origin, its stone-

Tithe Barn, Thame.

and-timbered brick walls were recently exposed in the course of refurbishment; its elegance is enhanced in early summer by a profusion of tapering pale violet racemes of wisteria cascading down the walls. In times past, the Stribblehill family were highly influential in the town and at one stage, through much of the seventeenth century, leased the Prebendal from the Thynne family. In the mid-sixteenth century, John Stribblehill, a leading churchwarden, had been, with his father Thomas, a supporter of King Henry VIII's policy towards the Church that excluded the papacy and brought the clergy more under state control, thus simultaneously strengthening the Crown's position and acquiring the monasteries' wealth.

Within sight of 'Stribblehills' is 'The Cruke', a sixteenth-century 'cruck' house, a type of construction more commonly found in deeper countryside. Cruck-framed building employed a simple construction with the roof and walls supported by pairs of arching A- shaped frames, each arm of the A formed from a split or curving trunk of oak or black poplar, together with a connecting roof tie. The crucks were likely to have been prepared off-site, perhaps in this case the Chilterns, prior to being assembled at the required site. The standard measurement between the crucks, or blades, as they are known in some parts of the country, was sixteen-and-a-half feet, or five-and-a-half yards, this being one rod, pole or perch, the old English measure mentioned earlier based on the amount of space needed to house two pairs of oxen.

Slightly closer to the town, a restaurant boasts 'Scheduled Ancient Building, *c.* 1550' as its origin. It is partly timbered, with magnificent chimneys. Closer still, is another sixteenth-century timber-framed building, Lancastrian Cottage, with a partially surviving cruck frame visible in the gable end. Fascinating as they may be, none of these buildings can claim to be the oldest structure in town. Not surprisingly, that honour has to go to the parish church dedicated to St Mary the Virgin. It was built of Headington stone in the mid-thirteenth century under the direction of Bishop Robert Grosseteste, who is thought to have been personally involved in both its design and its construction. The new building almost certainly necessitated the demolition of most of what would almost certainly have been a timber building, possibly the remnants of the earlier Anglo-Saxon church. We have mentioned a number of the bishops from this period, but Grosseteste was an exceptional character and is perhaps worthy of a little further examination, especially as he was so significant in the town's development.

Born around 1168, Robert Grosseteste was educated at Oxford University where he became proficient in law, medicine and the natural sciences. In 1215 he became one of its first Chancellors, remaining in post until about 1221. After this he held a number of ecclesiastical positions, and from 1229 to 1235 lectured in theology to the Franciscans at Greyfriars in Oxford. It was from around this time that he started to make his reputation as a theologian, and following the death of Hugh of Lincoln, he became Bishop of Lincoln in 1235, remaining in this position until his death in 1253.

Grosseteste was not just a theologian: he is still regarded as a crucially important figure in the history of English learning. He made Latin translations of many Greek and Arabic scientific writings, and wrote translations and commentaries of a number of Aristotle's newly discovered works. Nor did he just dabble in science: he conducted serious work on geometry, optics and astronomy, experimenting with mirrors and with lenses, and is hailed by some as the initiator of the English scientific tradition.

Like a number of his contemporary notables, Grosseteste was responsible for instigating the construction of a variety of substantial buildings, usually for ecclesiastical purposes, not least the Prebendal chapel and St Mary's church in Thame. What is perhaps more remarkable is the personal involvement he chose to exercise during the building of the church, given his advancing years over the duration of this particular church-building project.

The cruciform church is relatively large for the size of the town as it was at the time of its construction, and stands 'tall and grand, like a cathedral in miniature'.[61] In spite of the growth of the town over the centuries, the church still dominates the view of the town when approached from the north and west, no more so than at night time when floodlighting merely accentuates its commanding presence. Needless to say, it dwarfs the little dovecote, now a tool shed, in the churchyard.

Like so many churches, St Mary's includes work from just about every century since its construction in 1230–1240. The most recent restoration took place in 1991 when a reordering of the building also occurred. The principal changes involved replacing the nineteenth-century oak pews with locally made ash-wood chairs, and renewing the floor in the nave and aisles with Welsh slate and under-floor

St Mary's church, Thame, from the east.

heating. The changes were closely monitored by the Diocese of Oxford and English Heritage, but still met with a mix of enthusiasm and indignation among the local community, and not just from regular worshippers.

Removal of the nineteenth-century pipe organ and replacement with an electronic digital instrument exposed to better effect the delicate traceried fourteenth-century oak screen that had previously been somewhat obscured. Stonework restoration earlier in the twentieth century had revealed another treasure, a wall painting on the south-east pillar of the central tower. This pieta, showing Mary beneath the cross, with the dead body of Christ in her lap, had been hidden since 1548 when an order went out to 'white lyne' (lime) the church to wash out all medieval murals.

The nineteenth century had seen substantial work, including the removal of a number of galleries, but prior to that the church had languished in a generally poor state of repair for some 200 years. The church had been damaged by both opposing factions during the Civil War, and although some pressing repairs were carried out towards the end of the seventeenth century, including, for example, replacement oak doors in the south porch in 1682, the general condition was poor. Before that, the interior of the church had been much changed as a consequence of the Reformation, including removal of most of the ten or more altars that had previously been installed.

Prior to the Reformation, work on the structure of the building had continued since Grosseteste first built the church back in the thirteenth century. Conspicuously, the spire had been removed and in 1404 the tower was raised to its present height of ninety-five feet. The roof timbers are supported on oak posts that rest on corbels, six on each side of the nave. The subjects, all different and representing kings, men, women and angels, look down impassively on the nave and its congregation as they have done since they were fashioned in the fifteenth century.

The carved pulpit, like the altar table, is Jacobean and was originally part of a three-decker, whilst the font, with a simple leaf decoration, is at least 700-years-old. Its base is probably even older, and may even have come from the Saxon church that once stood on the same site. Its wooden cover is more modern – seventeenth century. Fonts were covered and usually locked to prevent theft of the holy water that was thought to have supernatural powers.

Around the church is the expected array of brasses and memorials, some with names now familiar to us – the Quartermains – Thomas, Richard and their families; and Geoffrey Dormer, his two wives and twenty-five children, for example. Like Richard Quartermain, Dormer came from a wealthy local family of merchants and landowners, and was himself a wool merchant of the staple of Calais. Other names are perhaps rather less familiar and include two early headmasters of Thame Grammar School, Edward Harris (the first headmaster and himself born in Thame) and Richard Boucher, who would have taught John Hampden. Francis Thynne (?1545-1608), who was a well-known Elizabethan alchemist, antiquary and herald, at one time a colleague of Camden at the College of Arms, and presumably a member of the Thynne family mentioned earlier, visited the church in 1582 and recorded the inscriptions of all the brasses. He had a curious blend of interests, for he was also a student of druidry and Egyptian magic! A brass of note, if only for its heraldry, commemorates the death of Sir John Clerk, a later owner of North Weston Manor who died in 1539. He was knighted for his exploits at the Battle of Spurs in 1513, when he was largely responsible for the capture of Louis of Orleans, Duke of Longueville. Clerk's first wife, who died in 1516, was Jane Lee, a member of the prominent Buckinghamshire family we met earlier. She was buried at Quarrendon chapel.

At the centre of the chancel is the marble tomb with its alabaster effigies of Lord Williams of Thame, who died in 1559, and his wife Elizabeth Bledlow, with greyhound and unicorn at their feet. The tomb was desecrated during the Civil War, and following repair, was put back facing west instead of east, contravening the usual practice of honouring the east end of the building.

In life, John Williams was also a somewhat unconventional character, not entirely popular it has to be said, though he was undoubtedly an astute man who managed to serve Henry VIII, Edward VI, Mary Tudor and Elizabeth I without, as one has put it, 'losing either his head or the immense fortune he had accumulated'.[62] He achieved this by means of a rather uncanny ability of accommodating himself to the prevailing religious culture without any loss of prestige or station, which for those times was quite an achievement. He is said to have acquired, by one means or another, some

Lord and Lady Williams' tomb, with attendant greyhound and unicorn, in St Mary's church, Thame.

twenty-eight estates that prior to the Dissolution had belonged to the Church. On his death, he did at least give back some of his accumulated gains to the people of Thame and its community by paying for the restoration of the almshouses and the founding of a grammar school. The original school building, close to the church, was erected in 1569 under the supervision of Marjorie Norreys, Williams's daughter, ten years after his death. The gabled stone building with its deep-mullioned windows is now the home of a commercial enterprise, a new school building having been provided along the Oxford Road in 1879.

Considering the size of the school, the alumni for the sixteenth, seventeenth and eighteenth centuries reads like a mini *Who's Who*, with a host of famous names from academia, politics, the church, arts and judiciary. In 1610, Camden described it as 'a very faire schoole';[63] such was its success and reputation in those early years that pupils were sent to the school from far and wide, though it was not always to be so. Harry Lupton, who went on to publish *The History of Thame and its Hamlets* in 1860, was at the school at a time when its success and popularity had dwindled to its lowest point, and there was only a handful of pupils, and a contemporary letter to the *Thame Gazette* described the school as, 'a richly endowed but comparatively useless Institution'.[64] From the earlier foundation years, however, there are too many illustrious names to list in full, though a few are worthy of mention, both for their fame and for some of the minor nuances of their lives.

Lord Williams's School, Thame. (Nineteenth-century print)

One of the first of the school's earlier pupils to come to national prominence was William Lenthall (1591-1662), Speaker of the so-called Long Parliament that was called by Charles I in 1640 and not formally dissolved until 1660. Being of a somewhat timorous nature, Lenthall was not entirely suited to the particularly turbulent nature of Parliament at the time, though he did once stand up to Charles I. Metaphorically, that is, as he was on his knees at the time, with the well-known words:

> May it please your Majesty, I have neither eyes to see nor tongue to speak in this place but as this House is pleased to direct me, whose servant I am here; and humbly beg your Majesty's pardon that I cannot give any other answer than this to what your Majesty is pleased to demand of me.[65]

The King had burst into Parliament to arrest five of its members in 1642. Never before had a reigning monarch entered the chamber, but they were unprecedented times, and Charles was to be thwarted anyway, for unbeknown to the King, the five had left the House by another route, having been forewarned of his intention. 'The Five Members', as they have come to be known, were John Pym, Arthur Haselrig, Denzil Holles, William Strode, and of course, John Hampden, of whom more anon.

Two old boys of the grammar school were among the group of regicides who had later participated in the trial and execution of Charles I. Simon Mayne (1612-1661)

1 Witchert building with thatch (Cuddington). Most structures are now topped with terracotta tiles.

2 Weir Lodge, Eythrope Estate.

3 'On stilly wings and forked tail'. The area's iconic red kite. (Photograph courtesy of Juan Piris)

4 Bird Cage Inn, Thame.

5 River Thame at site of former Notley Mill.

6 Autumn mists over the Thame at Shabbington.

7 River at Waterstock mill.

8 St Catherine and St Leonard church, Drayton St Leonard.

was eventually sentenced to death for his complicity in the events but died in the Tower of London before he could be executed. His co-conspirator, Sir Richard Ingoldsby (1615-1685), who lived near to Mayne in the hamlet of Waldridge, close by Lyde Brook, claimed he had been physically coerced into participation by Cromwell himself and was pardoned. Remarkably, he was allowed to retain the land he had acquired during the Protectorate, and resumed an active political life that spanned the reigns of Charles II and James II, outliving the less fortunate Mayne by nearly twenty-five years.

Mayne was born and lived a few miles out of Thame at Dinton Hall, where on at least one occasion he entertained Oliver Cromwell. After Mayne's death, his clerk, one John Bigg, went into a state of deep melancholy and lived out the rest of his own life in abject poverty in a cave (some say a shed) in Dinton, where his peculiar lifestyle earned him the title of the Dinton Hermit. There was speculation, that continued after his death in 1696, that he had had been the executioner of Charles I, though others argue that this is, 'without foundation for the deed was done with such accuracy and despatch that the executor was unlikely to have been an amateur'.[66]

For some, life went on in spite of the war, and Daniel Whistler (1619-1684), a few years younger than the regicides, seemingly devoted himself to saving life, rather than foreshortening it. He was born in Walthamstow, but educated at Lord Williams's School, and as a young physician, wrote an MD thesis at the University of Leyden on rickets (vitamin D deficiency) some five years before Glisson achieved eponymous fame with his description of what was regarded as an 'English' disease, in 1650. Later, Whistler became President of the Royal College of Physicians and was an early Fellow of the Royal Society. He was acquainted with Samuel Pepys who assessed him as, 'good company and a very ingenious man', and early in September 1666 at the time of the Great Fire of London, Pepys describes vividly how he, 'met with Mr. Young and Whistler; and ... they and I walked into the town . . . our feet ready to burn, walking through the towne among the hot coles'.[67]

It would seem that, in spite of Pepys' commendation, Whistler was not an entirely honourable man, and took advantage of his position as President of the Royal College of Physicians to defraud the College. In spite of this dubious activity and marriage to a rich widow, Whistler still 'died very much in debt, and worse than nothing',[68] suggesting that he was, perhaps, not the best role model to emerge from the school.

John Fell (1625-1686), on the other hand, became a renowned academic and churchman, at one time Bishop of Oxford, and according to fellow ex-Tamensian Anthony Wood, 'the most zealous man of his time for the Church of England'.[69] Fell was a strict disciplinarian, and it was not unknown, for example, for him to personally visit the local taverns and order students to leave the premises. Little wonder, then, that as a result of a run-in over an academic matter with one particular errant student he became the subject of the well-known axiom, 'I do not love thee,

Dr Fell, The reason why I cannot tell, But this I know, and know full well, I do not love thee, Dr Fell', this being the student's extempore translation of the Latin epigram, *Non amo te, Sabidi, nec possum dicere – quare: Hoc tantum possum dicere, non amo te.*[70]

The student, incidentally, was Thomas Brown (1663-1704), later to achieve some modest fame in his own right as a satirist, Tory pamphleteer and hack writer. Fell too is also remembered in a literary connection, as a vigorous supporter and promoter, both practically and financially, of the Oxford University Press.

The aforementioned Anthony Wood (1632-1695) devoted his adult life to antiquarian studies, though he was a man of many interests. When aged twenty, for example, he took up ploughing, but his greatest relaxation was derived from music and particularly playing the violin and bell-ringing. Perhaps his interest in the latter was sparked off while he lived so close to Thame church that in 1675 had at least six bells, though bell-ringing in Thame went back considerably further than Wood's time. In 1512, when Henry VIII passed through the town, the bell-ringers were given ale in recognition of their peal of welcome. Henry returned to Thame in 1530, accompanied by Catherine of Aragon and his next wife, Anne Boleyn who was then a lady-in-waiting. There are records of recastings of Thame's bells going back to this same year but they are unclear as to the total number of bells. As well as their use for ceremonial and processional purposes, church bells had a sacramental use within the liturgy, but with the introduction of the *Book of Common Prayer*, Thomas Cranmer effectively abolished the ringing of the bells for the dead. The ringers at Thame rang a defiant peal at the Feast of All Saints in 1549, however, giving some indication of the town's conservatism. In his capacity as Sheriff of Oxfordshire, incidentally, Lord Williams was present in Oxford in 1556 when Cranmer was burnt at the stake, having been found guilty of heresy. Contemporary accounts record that when Cranmer began his final address, Williams impatiently told him to 'Make short, make short'.[71] Today, Cranmer is of course regarded more as the creator of the English reformed church than the heretic he was once branded.

Anthony Wood, or Anthony à Wood as he later liked to be known, was a pupil at Lord Williams's school at the time of the Civil War, when the nearby church was used for all sorts of activity – barracks, stables, prison, hospital – that resulted in considerable damage to the building, and his studies were inevitably disrupted by occasional skirmishes between Royalist and Parliamentarian forces. He lodged at the vicarage, close to the church, and just a few hundred yards from the school, and wrote (in the third person, as was his custom) that, 'you cannot imagine what disturbance they [Anthony and his brother Christopher, younger by three years] suffered by the soldiers of both parties, sometimes by parliament's soldiers of Aylesbury, sometimes by the King's from Boarstall House and at Oxon. and at Wallingford Castle'.[72]

The vicarage was probably only a few yards from the strategic Crendon Bridge, and perhaps from the vantage point of their temporary home, the young Wood brothers regularly witnessed fierce clashes and the horrors of war, 'They saw a great number of horsemen posting towards Thame over Crendon Bridge … and in the head of them was [Colonel Thomas] Blagge [Governor of Wallingford Castle] with a bloody face.' On another occasion they watched as, 'Captain Bunce [one of Prince Rupert's captains] charged over the (mill) bridge, and with his pistols shot one of (the rebel Parliamentarians) dead'. A broad curriculum for the young lads, indeed. Later, in June 1646, the Boarstall garrison surrendered to Parliament and the scholars were, 'allowed by their master a free liberty [holiday] and many went thither (four miles distant) … to see the form of the surrender'.[73]

Thomas Ellwood (1639-1714), son of a one-time Lord Mayor of London, was born close to Thame at nearby Crowell. He would scarcely have been old enough to have such vivid recollections of the Civil War, but at school, he was by his own admission a bit of a rascal. In *The History of the Life of Thomas Ellwood: Written by Himself*, he claimed that, 'few boys in [Lord Williams's] school wore out more birch than I' not because of any lack of academic achievement, but because he 'was often playing some waggish prank among my fellow scholars'.[74] His premature removal from the school (for financial reasons) clearly saddened him, describing the experience as, 'something like plucking green fruit from the tree and laying it by before it was due to come to ripeness, when it will therefore shrink and wither, and lose that little juice and relish which it begun to have'.[75]

Surprising, perhaps, that this self-confessed prankster should later defy his father to become a committed member of the early Quaker movement, and a close friend of its founder, George Fox. He also became a friend of John Milton, and helped him to find the property that Ellwood described as 'that pretty box in St Giles, Chalfont',[76] now a Grade I Listed sixteenth-century building, where Milton, by then blind and with his third wife, could escape plague-ridden London. It was there, too, that a chance comment by Ellwood inspired Milton to write, by means of painstaking dictation, *Paradise Regained*, the sequel to his more famous *Paradise Lost*.

After he left Lord Williams's School, Sir John Holt (1642-1710), who was born in Thame at the outset of the Civil War, studied law and was called to the Bar in 1663. He was a prominent counsel in the State trials of his day, and rose to become Lord Chief Justice of the King's Bench under William III. As a judge he stood in stark contrast to most of his predecessors, having an impressive reputation for uncompromising fairness and integrity, clarity of expression, all underpinned by an undisputed extensive legal knowledge. Always an impassioned supporter of civil and religious liberty, he is well remembered for a willingness to oppose the authority of Parliament in order to uphold his perception of justice. His approach to the Establishment has the ring of a modern-day television courtroom drama series.

Having some ideals in common with Holt, but campaigning in rather different style, John Wilkes (1727-1797) was to become a radical journalist and politician, a supporter of William Pitt the Elder, and perhaps best remembered for his supporters' cry of 'Wilkes and Liberty'. He undoubtedly received some of his education in Thame, though there is some disagreement as to whether this was at Lord

Williams's School or another establishment under the aegis of the newly formed Presbyterian meeting-house. Wilkes was a man of wit, learning and ability who was also something of a rake and a member of High Wycombe's Hellfire Club, though this did not prevent election to Parliament – he was at one time MP for Aylesbury – or to the position of Lord Mayor of London. His ready wit was legendary. In one of the most famous extempore put-downs of all time, Wilkes deflated the Earl of Sandwich who had jeered at him, 'Wilkes, you will die either on the gallows or of the pox.' Wilkes reply was simple, 'That depends, my Lord, on whether I embrace your Lordship's principles – or your mistress'![77]

Wilkes's ability to summon up a ready riposte was shared with a rather earlier pupil, the poet Edmund Waller (1606-1687). Born into a family of wealthy landowners, Waller was probably educated at Lord Williams's school before moving on to Eton and King's College, Cambridge, becoming a Member of Parliament at the tender age of sixteen. He was born, incidentally, just forty days before the introduction of the first Union Flag. It consisted of the red cross of St George and the white on blue cross of St Andrew, the diagonal red cross of St Patrick not being incorporated until 1801. During the turbulent years of the 1640s, Waller declined to nail his own colours to the mast and continued to steer a moderate course between the King and his opponents in Parliament. Later, at a time to suit his purpose, he wrote panegyrics to both Cromwell and Charles II, and upon Charles' suggestion that Cromwell's was the better poem, Waller is said to have replied, 'Sir, we poets never succeed so well in writing truth as in fiction'.[78]

No such vacillation from John Hampden (1594-1643), the school's most illustrious old boy and the 'Patriot' whose stand against Charles I by refusing to pay Ship Money on his land in Stoke Mandeville effectively precipitated the country into Civil war. Ship Money was a tax used to fund the navy that traditionally had been only raised in counties with a coastline, not inland counties such as Buckinghamshire. Having lighted the blue touch paper, as it were, Hampden did not withdraw to watch the fireworks, but threw himself personally into the conflict, and therein met his untimely death, paying the ultimate price for his principles. All of his contemporaries praised John Hampden's character and capabilities. Even a Royalist opponent, The Earl of Clarendon, conceded that, 'his reputation for honesty was universal, and his affections seemed so publicly guided that no corrupt or private ends could bias them', and that, 'he was a very wise man, and of great parts, and possessed with the most absolute faculties to govern the people, of any man I knew'.[79] In later years the writer and politician Edmund Burke asked, 'Would twenty shillings [the cost of his Ship Money] have ruined Mr Hampden's fortune? No, but the payment of half twenty shillings on the principle it was demanded, would have made him a slave'.[80] And so it happened that quite early on in the war, Hampden rode out from Thame to challenge some of Prince Rupert's soldiers returning to Oxford from a sortie towards High Wycombe. Although he held the bridge, Rupert feared he would be cornered in a bottleneck at the crossing over the River Thame at Chiselhampton, and so turned to repel the challenge, and in the skirmish that followed, Hampden was severely wounded in the shoulder, possibly shot accidentally by his own faulty weapon. He managed to ride back to Thame, and sought refuge in the Greyhound Inn (now a shop building known as Hampden House) where Ezekiel Brown resided, and where he was attended by his friend Dr Giles, the Rector of Chinnor. Sadly, he died from his injury six days later, an event now commemorated by a marble memorial on a wall nearby.

Our journey along the River Thame is peppered with tales of soldiers and of wars, clearly nowhere more so than in Thame itself, geographically and strategically close to the heart of the Civil War, as we have just seen. One writer has suggested that, 'during the troubled years of the Civil War Thame was England in microcosm'.[81] However, our glimpse into the history of this little town must surely make mention of a warrior to be found in a rather different arena, the boxer James Figg. Born in Thame in 1695, he became Great Britain's first bare-knuckle boxing champion in 1719, retiring as undefeated champion in 1730. His retirement was unfortunately rather short-lived, for he was to die only ten years later. He allegedly suffered only one defeat in his 271 fights, at a time when boxing was a rather different sport than in our own days, with no ring, no rounds, no referee, and effectively no rules. Invariably fighting as 'James Figg of Thame', he also claimed the title of 'Master of the noble science of defence', and was skilled in fencing as well as boxing, running a flourishing school in London, where he taught techniques of both armed and unarmed combat. Such was his success and renown that the Prime Minister of his day, Sir Robert Walpole, attended at least one of his fights, and the literature advertising his school was designed by no less than the later famed artist William Hogarth. Now his memory lives on, revived by the recent renaming of one of the town's many public houses as 'Jimmy Figg's'.

Thame has something of a reputation for its public houses – fifty-nine are recorded over the centuries, though the figure is probably somewhat inflated due to name changes by some establishments that are thus counted twice. In 1906 there were thirty-five, three times the county average for the population! Dr Robert Plot (1640-1696) was an energetic, some would say quaint, Oxford academic, well versed in a range of subjects but especially natural history. He set out to write a county-by-county record of natural history but managed to complete volumes only for Oxfordshire and Staffordshire, though even the first of these was enough to earn him thereafter the title 'the learned Dr Plot'. He had a poor view of the water that flowed through Thame, and the wells that supplied it with water, claiming that it was so impregnated with sulphur that beer turned to a noxious compound in the space of fourteen days. A challenge for the town's many landlords, it would seem!

Having come full circle and back to the subject of water, it is perhaps time to resume our journey and continue downstream towards our final destination. However, we cannot leave Thame without mention of one further location nearby, with close ties to the town and its people.

Thame Park, lying about a mile and a half to the south east of the town, is an area of some 300 acres that has been enclosed since Saxon times. The present eighteenth-century house, with its added Palladian frontage, is built on the site of a twelfth-century Cistercian abbey, which had been relocated from the Otmoor village of Oddington. The abbey received favours from Henry III by way of grants and tax concessions, but even before the Dissolution, things – both structural and moral – had started to deteriorate. After the Dissolution, the last Abbot, one Robert King, whose brother was brother-in-law to Sir John Williams, became the first Bishop of Oxford, and the manorial lands were given to Sir John (in the right place at the right time, again!). A later owner was Sir Richard Wenman, who was suspected of complicity in the gunpowder plot of 1605, though nothing was ever proven, and indeed he was subsequently promoted to Viscount Wenman.

In the early 1960s, the author went to the park on several occasions with a few others, to take Sunday afternoon tea with the then owner's son, a fellow Boy Scout, and was, needless to say, quite oblivious to all this history. The greater concern was an apprehension of meeting the 'pet' cheetah that allegedly was allowed to roam free in the grounds. It was never encountered unchained, needless to say. The Park acquired a rather wider audience in later years through its use for location shots for films such as *Saving Private Ryan* and *The Madness of King George.*

five

Shabbington to Waterstock

then they procéed togither as one by Shabbington, Ricot parke, Dracot, Waterstoke ...

From Thame, the river flows westward towards the little village of Shabbington, still passing through flat meadows so liable to spectacular flooding when the rainfall is excessive. It was across these fields between Thame and Shabbington that as a schoolboy, the author experienced, somewhat reluctantly, the, 'joys' of cross-country running, wading through the river on the way out and again, a little upstream, on the home run. In an earlier era, and well before the luxury of swimming pools, indoor or outdoor, schoolchildren in Thame received their 'official' swimming lessons in the river; for some, in the late nineteenth century at least, this was at Jemmett's Hole, where in later years the treasure was found. For generations, mostly prior to the advent of PlayStations and DVDs, and before parents became so concerned about the safety and security of their children, Jemmett's Hole, an extended loop in the river just to the north of the Prebendal and towards Shabbington, was a favoured spot for swimming and generally 'messing about'. Also known as 'The Basin', it has the inevitable abundance of willows, reeds and rushes, from which an occasional heron may be disturbed, startled by human intrusion from its patient vigil at water's edge.

In summer, a prominent growth of Himalayan balsam (*Impatiens glandulifera*) is conspicuous along the river's southern bank, either side of 'The Basin'. It is a vigorously growing plant, with flowers varying in colour from white through pale to deep rose pink, and by attaining a height of up to six feet, is one of the tallest 'wild' flowers in Britain. Botanically, it is related to the ever popular, and very much smaller, 'busy Lizzie', though in reality it is an alien invader, introduced into the country from Asia as a cultivated species in 1839. A colloquial name is 'jumping Jack,' a name given because of the way the ripe seed capsules explode so readily, each releasing up to twelve seeds that may be flung as far away as fifteen feet, and by landing on land or water, allow the plant to spread easily along stream and river margins. An average plant may produce as many as 2,500 seeds in total, and the species has become so 'successful' in Britain that it is now regarded as something of a nuisance. Dense, vigorously growing clumps prevent light reaching shorter, native plants that then struggle to survive, whilst its presence increases the risk of riverbank erosion because it similarly precludes the growth of perennial plants such as grasses, which bind the soil with their roots; when the annual balsam plants die in the

Second bridge over the Thame at Shabbington, towards Thame.

autumn they leave bare patches of soil, which can be more readily washed away by rain, destabilising the riverbank.

Children have come to this part of the river since well before the time this particular plant became established here, however, and bearing in mind the pedigree of some former pupils of local schools, one must presume indeed that, 'the toes of the famous have puddled and paddled in its [the Thame's] cool waters and along its intriguing margins'.[82] For many youngsters in and around the town, famous-to-be or otherwise, the waters of the Thame provided an opportunity for a bit of excitement, for bravado and daring, and even occasionally, when the river was flooded and faster flowing, for dicing with danger, as the *Bucks Village Boy*[83] has vividly described.

Just before the river reaches Shabbington, it divides and both arms turn sharply southward past the village and its church. Built on a low ridge, the little church of St Mary Magdalene is set back from the main road through the village that at this point runs generally parallel to the river. It is a stone building with a tiled roof and a low embattled tower from the fifteenth century. The main part of the church is Norman, characterised by some medieval herringbone stonework. The panelled hexagonal pulpit is Jacobean, and below the plastered roof of the nave are tie beams dating back to the era of the Wars of the Roses. Even the gentry of rural Oxfordshire was not immune to the latter conflict, incidentally, and Richard Quartermain, for example, (or Quatremayns as his name is sometimes spelt), the wealthy landowner from neighbouring North Weston who built Rycote chapel and Thame's almshouse, personally fought in the war.

Buildings in the rest of the village are a blend of ages and styles, with few that are really old. Yet the church is not the only evidence that hints at the age of the settlement here. The village was recorded in the Domesday Book of 1062 as Sobintone (an Anglo-Saxon name meaning 'Scobba's farm') and subsequently became known as Shobbington, only changing to Shabbington in relatively recent Victorian times. There is record of a mill, where the Old Fisherman restaurant now stands, as well as a post-medieval fishery, with eels a major commodity, and a decoy pond. The road running from the main village, past the church and towards the restaurant, is even today known as Mill Road, a legacy to former activity, whilst fields nearby still show the characteristic ridge and furrow formations born of even earlier medieval agricultural activity.

Both streams of the river are bridged at Shabbington near the Old Fisherman, at the south end of the village, just as the road to Thame turns through a right-angled bend. The two bridges are very different in character: the one nearer to the restaurant is a fairly mundane, mostly concrete affair, but the other, further away from the village and scarcely noticeable to the motorist apart from a constriction to the road and a slight hump, is an attractive, two-arched red-brick structure. Walkways between the bridges and on the approach from the Thame side are raised for some distance, an indication of the frequency and severity of the floods to which the area is prone, though even these structures are at times insufficient to keep the pedestrian totally dry. It is a pretty spot, nonetheless, and like a number of towns and villages in the area, has attracted the attention of television filmmakers, notably as a location for the popular *Midsomer Murders* series.

A few miles to the north east of Shabbington, and now associated by little more than a shared name, is Shabbington Wood. This area is the largest remaining woodland relict of the ancient Bernwood Forest that had its roots as a hunting forest from the early tenth century, when it was known as Barne Wood. Edward the Confessor, who was born not so far away at Islip, put Bernwood on the map, as it were, and built a hunting lodge-cum-palace at Brill for his use when on hunting visits. By the time of Henry II, Bernwood Forest formed part of an almost contiguous swathe of woodland that stretched from Oxford to Stamford Bridge. Over ensuing centuries, political and financial pressures forced successive monarchs to disafforest the land, though when the forest was at its greatest extent, Shabbington was one of the many parishes that fell on or within its boundaries, and the River Thame itself formed both a natural and administrative boundary at the south of the forest.

Nowadays only a relatively small area of woodland remains, and interest centres more on conservation than the rather destructive, albeit necessary activities of the Middle Ages. The wood is designated a Site of Special Scientific Interest, not least because of the rich variety of butterflies that are to be found. Some forty species have been recorded in the last decade or so, revealing a spectrum of colours, and including occasional sightings of the clouded yellow and holly blue, the elusive purple emperor, the less widespread silver-washed fritillary, and the rare black hairstreak. There is of course, more to the wood than its butterflies, and its mixed population of conifer and broad-leaved trees is home to an interesting range of flora and fauna. An extensive selection of resident and visiting birds may be seen, including two perhaps less commonly spotted in this area, the woodcock and crossbill. The woodcock's highly effectively camouflaged plumage makes it extremely difficult to locate, as an old adage says:

For fools are known by looking wise,
as men find woodcock by their eyes.[84]

It is a mostly nocturnal, and altogether rather strange-looking bird, its large eyes placed such that their rear vision is more effective than their forward vision. The crossbill, a winter visitor and frequenter of mature coniferous forests and plantations, is also distinctive, with a curious bill marking it out as a specialist feeder of conifer seeds, in particular larch, fir and spruce.

At times, when the lingering warmth of summer blends with the dampening air of autumn, the forest provides rich rewards for fungi 'forayers'. As a rule, fungi thrive in moist areas rich in decaying organic material from which they can draw their nutrients, and the woods here are ideal for supporting the wide variety of shapes, colours and sometimes odours of these curious plant forms, that range from being edible to being highly poisonous. Like butterflies, they have intriguing, sometimes bizarre names, and the woods here are host to, amongst others, stinkhorn and puffball, fairy stool and penny button, not to mention ink caps and a variety of bracket fungi.

Fallow and muntjac deer roam the woods. The former, along with red deer and roe deer, were commonplace in Edward's time, being valued as a major source of food, of course. Paradoxically, they were at certain times protected by their hunters: cattle grazing was allowed in the open spaces of the Forest, provided the King's deer were not disturbed, but was barred for the two weeks before and after midsummer when the deer were fawning.

Muntjac, strictly speaking a species called Reeves' muntjac, is a relatively recent addition to the list of Britain's wild animals. Also known as the Barking deer because of its characteristic rather high-pitched barking alarm call, it was introduced to the country from the Far East in the late nineteenth century by the Duke of Bedford. It is widely accepted that the muntjac we now see in increasing numbers in the wild, and sadly also as road-kill, are the successive progeny of escapees from the Duke's Woburn estate and more recently from Whipsnade Zoo. There is a downside to their presence, however: muntjacs destroy the low-cover nesting habitat of a variety of birds and are blamed for the decline of several resident species. The seventy per cent reduction in the number of nightingales in Oxfordshire and Buckinghamshire over the last twenty years, for example, has been attributed largely to the concurrent increase in muntjac.

Away from the forest, and shortly past the restaurant at the edge of Shabbington village, the two branches of the river converge, just before the river commences a significant curve to the right which takes it on a course that runs about half a mile to the south of Ickford. For a while it runs close to the Thame to Oxford road, from where swans may sometimes be seen in adjacent fields quite some distance from the river, perhaps enjoying the lush meadow grass or cereal crops, or even foraging for worms or other delicacies as a change from their usual diet of underwater plants. The gently flowing River Thame is of course an ideal environment for these graceful creatures, but there is a potential downside. As swans ingest grit to help them digest their food, they sometimes accidentally ingest pieces of lead and other items discarded negligently or wantonly by fishermen. The toxic lead breaks down in their stomachs and causes muscular and nervous damage. Affected swans have kinked necks because muscle tissue becomes too weak to support their necks properly, and flight and aerial navigational skills may be impaired. Lead fishing weights have been banned in Britain for some time, but inevitably there must be some left at the bottoms of rivers that could still be churned up and ingested by a swan.

Angling is one of the country's most popular recreational activities and it would be wrong to tar all anglers with the same brush, of course, and later on we will refer in a little greater detail to some of the more positive aspects of this popular pastime on the Thame. The sport was equally popular in Lupton's time, when there were fears that the waters around Thame had been over-fished, or as he himself wrote, that fishing had 'sadly thinned the finney tribe'.[85] Anthony Wood similarly was a recreational fisherman. Would these pupils of the old grammar school, albeit separated by the best part of 200 years, have raised an eyebrow to find that angling is now on their old school's alternative curriculum? As well as the theory and practice of angling, pupils learn the core subjects of English, mathematics and science, 'with a fishy twist',[86] during their innovative eight- week course.

Passing so close, we cannot ignore Rycote chapel, a building that is actually something of a jewel in Oxfordshire's crown. Rycote, once a significant Anglo-Saxon settlement west of Thame, is little more than half-a-mile from the downward loop of the River Thame due south of Shabbington. At the time of the Domesday Book, Rycote already had a manor that was later to be modified into a great Tudor Palace, built on the lines of Hampton Court Palace, possibly by Lord Williams of Thame. The palace was honoured at various times by visits from royalty. Henry VIII honeymooned there in 1540 with wife number five, Catherine Howard. Queen Elizabeth was a regular guest, both as a child, as a 'prisoner', and later when Queen, enjoying a long and close friendship with Henry Norreys and his wife Marjorie, Lord Williams' daughter, who had inherited the palace from her father. James I visited, as did Charles I at the time of an outbreak of plague in London, when the royal court temporarily relocated to Oxford. The palace was destroyed, and the heir

Ancient yew tree near Rycote chapel.

to the property killed by fire in 1745, and though initially refurbished, it had been largely dismantled by the turn of the century, with only the stable block, now a private house, remaining. A more recent owner, Captain Michaelis, was instrumental in the foundation of Rycotewood College in the 1930s.

Richard Quartermain had acquired the manor in 1415, the year of the Battle of Agincourt, and he set about construction of Rycote Chapel, designed for private use and consecrated in 1449. Unlike the manor house, this little chapel has survived mostly unchanged, apart from the addition of two extraordinary wooden pews, thought to have been installed for the visit of Charles I in 1625, at the time when King and Parliament moved to Oxford to escape the plague. The two large pews, one either side of the aisle, are like small rooms, with exquisitely carved delicate fretwork and screening walls. One, the family pew, has two storeys with its own wooden stairs; the other, the royal pew, has a curious dome, decorated with stars on a blue background.

The chapel's superb wagon-vaulted roof is original 1449, and the font even older, the whole premises being quite unique in the county and probably the country. Just outside the chapel is a massive ancient yew tree, as tall as the chapel tower and now said to measure twenty-six feet in circumference, and allegedly brought from Palestine, and planted at the time of King Stephen's coronation in 1135. Local legend says it was used as a pilgrim marker on the nearby Oxfordshire Way. The 'learned Dr Plot' had some words to say about another remarkable tree at Rycote:

> And at Ricote in the park of the Right Honourable the Lord Norreys, there was a Oak which extends its Branches from the Trunk of the Tree about 18 yds, so that the Diameter of its circumference being 36 yds, it takes within its area 972 sq yds; under the Umbrage of which Tree, upon the afore mentioned Proportions, no less than 324 horses, or 4374 Men may sufficiently be sheltered.[87]

A monster indeed, though clearly not as massive as the spread oak in Worksop Park that allegedly could 'shelter 1,000 horse'.[88] Rycote's yew, meanwhile, offers more than enough cover for its resident nesting goldcrests, Britain's smallest bird.

The road that bridges the river below Ickford was once of greater significance than it now enjoys, being part of the direct route from Milton Common, on the London to Oxford road, to Bernwood Forest and particularly to Edward's medieval palace at Brill. There was a crossing here at least as far back as 1237, when Walter de Burgh was ordered to provide the bridge keeper with a single oak from the wood of Brohull (Brill) with which to carry out essential repairs. Leland described a stone bridge of two arches, with a secondary wooden bridge. The latter was subsequently replaced with a stone bridge to allow floodwater through the causeway. The main stone bridge is certainly seventeenth century – it bears a weathered inscription '1685 Here ends the county of Oxon' on the Tiddington side, and 'Here Begineth the county of Bucks 1685' on the Ickford side – and there is a possibility that, though modified in 1685, the bridge itself was built rather earlier, and may indeed be the structure described by Leland. The main structure includes two triangular retreats for pedestrians that are carried down to form cutwaters. It is a steeply humped, narrow bridge that affords only restricted visibility for motorists, ensuring, in spite of the recesses, a rather perilous crossing for any intrepid, or careless, pedestrians. The adjacent floodwater Whirlpool Arch, which is itself a Grade II Listed monument that dates back to 1824, when it was rebuilt after the original stone structure was destroyed by floods, was again partially demolished around the time of writing in 2006, this time after a car apparently crashed through the parapet.

We have already seen that the history of the River Thame is interspersed with battles, particularly during the years of the Civil War, but also probably back to earlier times in British history. According to Camden, Ickford, called Yttingaford by the Saxons, was the place of a treaty between King Alfred and the Danes in AD 907, presumably as a result of some potential or actual conflict. Close to the bridge at Ickford, however, another battle is still fought. Since the year of Queen Elizabeth II's Coronation, the villagers of Ickford have engaged those of Tiddington in an annual tug-of-war contest across the width of the river (about forty-eight feet at this point) at a spot where it is still the county boundary. Clearly, the losers get a soaking, but sadly for the spectators, the contest rarely lasts for more than three or four minutes!

On a windowsill in the north aisle of the little church of St Nicholas, there is evidence of yet another rivalry, in the shape of the markings of the ancient game of

Flooded meadows near Ickford Bridge.

Tug of war, Ickford, 1987. (Photograph courtesy of *The Thame Gazette*)

Nine Men's Morris. Also known variously around the country as Morrelles, Merrills, Merels, Mill, Morris, even Meg Merrylegs, Nine Men's Marriage or Ninepenny, the game is thought to derive from Egypt, around 1400 BC. Its popularity peaked in England in the Middle Ages, when the 'board' for the game would be scraped out on village greens, chalked out on slates in taverns, and evidently also scratched out on church windowsills! Today, inevitably perhaps, it has been taken up by the massive computer-game industry, a far cry from ancient Egypt, or even Shakespeare's brief mention of the game in *A Midsummer Night's Dream*, when Titania observes that, 'The Nine Men's Morris is filled up with mud'.[89] Clearly there were some advantages in playing the game indoors!

Elsewhere in the church, a single arch is the only remaining structure from the original Norman building; most of the remainder is thirteenth century. Gilbert Sheldon (1598-1677) was rector here from 1636-1660, some time before he became Archbishop of Canterbury (1663), or before he built at his own expense the Sheldonian Theatre in Oxford (1669), or, shortly before his death, he assisted Christopher Wren with the reconstruction of St Paul's Cathedral.

From Ickford Bridge, the Thame continues in a north-westerly direction for a mile or so, and then does a sharp U-turn, taking a south-easterly direction past Waterperry and on to Waterstock, whereupon it turns ninety degrees and heads towards the M40 motorway.

The name Waterperry comes from the Old English *pirie*, meaning 'pear tree', and *pereium*, meaning 'pear orchard'. Waterperry is a secluded village situated on the flood plain of the Thame, which runs across the south of the village, with Holton Brook as its western boundary. Vehicular access to the village is possible only from one end, and the single street, with its curious mix of relatively new council houses and seventeenth and eighteenth-century cottages, some timber framed and built of coarse stone or brick, terminates near Waterperry House, a Georgian building that now lies at the heart of a flourishing garden centre.

Within the grounds of the house, which was itself probably built on the site of a medieval house existing before 1086, is Waterperry's parish church of St Mary the Virgin, 'an architectural treasure trove',[90] with remnants of a Saxon arch clearly visible inside. The canopied, three-decker pulpit dates from the seventeenth century, and old high-backed box pews date similarly from Jacobean times. Some retain original ornate hinges, and brass candlesticks, now converted to electric light, adorn the tops of the pews. It is claimed that few small churches can boast such an array of outstanding old glass, stretching over four centuries. The oldest, in the three lancet windows on the north side of the chancel, has been dated to around 1220. It comes from a period when the richly coloured glass of the twelfth century gave way for a time to 'grisaille', delicately coloured glass with simple designs that were painted on.

There are brasses, too, and though by no means the oldest in the church, the palimpsest brass in the nave is well known. It was first used in 1440, laid in a church

Tranquillity at Waterperry.

in Leadenhall Street, London, in memory of a city couple, Simon and Margareta Kamp. At the time of the Reformation it was sold, and later re-fashioned, with appropriate changes in the attire of the figures from the fashion of the Lancastrian era to that of Tudor times, for Walter and Isabel Curson, who died in the earlier part of the sixteenth century. The motive for recycling the brass may have been financial rather than conservationist, but clearly such measures are not the exclusive invention of modern 'green' campaigners. The commemoration is slightly curious, as the Curson family remained staunchly Catholic after the Reformation, and were on the official list of recusants, even harbouring at Waterperry for a while Sir Edward Warpole, a Jesuit priest. The Cursons, and before them the FitzElys (or FitzEllis), and after them the Henleys, dominated the village for many generations: little wonder really that there are memorials to them all in the church. Perhaps the most beautiful is the FitzElys effigy underneath a remarkable canopy, one of the country's finest examples of mid-fourteenth-century English sculpture.

One of the other unique features of the church is its old wooden, weather-boarded tower, the timber now looking rather weary and neglected. The turret rests on massive oak pillars and an arch inside the church, and is something of a rarity, certainly for Oxfordshire.

Though there is only the one no-through-road into the village, there is a pedestrian back-door link to neighbouring Waterstock via a bridleway over the brick-built Bow Bridge, set over the little stream known as Black Ditch that was

Bow Bridge, Waterstock.

formerly the bypass stream for Waterstock Mill on the River Thame. The present bridge was built in 1790 by Diana Ashurst, and comprises a single arch with solid, out-curving stone parapets. There is occasional reference to a previous structure here called Lincroft Bridge, dating back to the twelfth century.

Waterstock Mill itself is certainly mentioned in the Domesday Book. Originally, the present house was a fifteenth-century brick-and-timber building, but was rebuilt in the Elizabethan period. It was converted into a modern dwelling in the 1950s, around the time that the feudal 'squirearchy', with latterly the Ashurst family at its head, gradually relaxed its hold on the village.

The name 'Waterstock', meaning 'watering place', suggests Anglo-Saxon origins, and nearby ridge and furrow formations indicate a medieval settlement. Remarkably, it is thought that the population of the village is much the same in number now as it was some 800 years ago. Set along the single street that runs through the village are a variety of cottages, one of which is a cruck house of medieval origins. St Leonard's church also has its derivation in that era, though it has been substantially rebuilt on several occasions since, most recently when its unusual bellcote was restored. In 2000, the village commissioned a local stained-glass artist to produce a Millennium Window, a representation of the tree and river of life, incorporating also the ancient Christian symbol of the fish.

Rather older is the canopied memorial inside the church that commemorates a former pupil, and one of the earliest, of Lord Williams's School that we have not mentioned previously. Sir George Croke (1560–1641) was born in Chilton and went on to become a justice of the King's Bench. His legal arguments outlived him, and are quoted by lawyers even today. He resisted Royal interference with the Courts, and participated in the 'Ship Money' trial that saw John Hampden sentenced to imprisonment. Croke's rhetoric persuaded both Houses of Parliament to vote against the judgement, so securing Hampden's release. He was not above more parochial matters also, and like several local notables we have encountered, Croke founded a chapel and almshouses in the area, and when later he retired, he took up residence in Waterstock where he lived until his death.

Croke's grandfather, who had worked in royal service, built the manor house at Chilton, and following the Dissolution, purchased Studley Priory, a property that stayed in the family for many generations, whilst his brother Robert at one stage owned Chequers, a property later bought by descendants of the Lee dynasty, and now the official country residence of the Prime Minister. By coincidence, the Prime Minister's London residence in Downing Street, stands on the site of John Hampden's London home, which was built by Sir Thomas Knyvet in the 1580s and inherited by Hampden's mother in 1622, when her son was twenty-eight. At this time he was an MP and so would almost certainly have lived at the property when in London. Members of the John Hampden Society believe that it is a disgrace that, for over 300 years, the official residence of the Head of Government of the United Kingdom should be named after a man such as Sir George Downing. Downing (1623–1684), who accrued the basis of a family fortune to which Downing College, Cambridge, owes its existence, was a politician and diplomat of remarkable energy, ruthlessness and ambition, and his unscrupulousness was notorious. The John Hampden Society regards him as 'a turncoat and hypocrite',[91] and has lobbied government officials, thus far unsuccessfully, to rename Downing Street in honour of their hero.

Less controversially, there are inside Waterstock church a number of memorials to the Ashurst family, including a genealogy window comprising forty-five shields, whilst their patronage of the church is recorded on a brass panel that lists against a time line all the monarchs, Bishops of Lincoln, and Rectors of Waterstock and their patrons since 1235. Close by the church is the old Ashurst family home, Waterstock House. The present building actually comprises just the stables and servants' quarters of the original eighteenth-century house, most of the rest of which was demolished in the 1950s, and functions as a riding and training centre of some repute.

Just outside the village, but sharing its name, is a golf course and driving range of recent origins whose land stretches down at one point almost to the banks of the Thame. The golf course is within sight, and at times earshot, of the stretch of M40 motorway extension that was engineered passed Wheatley and on towards Birmingham in 1991, narrowly missing Otmoor, with its 'magical tranquillity',[92] a few miles to the north-west of the River Thame.

Planning for the stretch of motorway from Waterstock to Birmingham began in 1973, and gave rise to two 'firsts' in motorway construction. The process included the first ever public consultation held for a road building scheme, and took ten years to decide on the final route, with the Otmoor factor a major sticking-point, and quite rightly so, many would argue. Otmoor, likened to, 'a languorous East Anglian fen transplanted into the heart of Oxfordshire',[93] and said to be, 'one of the last open wildernesses left in Britain',[94] is a nature reserve of wet meadows and reed beds, a haven in winter for thousands of waterfowl, including teal and widgeon, a hunting ground for owls, merlin and harrier, and a home in spring and summer for songbirds – including a variety of warblers and nightingales – and breeding wading birds, such as lapwing, curlew and plover. Even before the advent of the motorway, the area had been 'developed', with serious loss of natural habitat. Now organisations such as the RSPB are working hard to restore some of these losses, and are optimistic for the future. Even the elusive bittern, that 'cryptically camouflaged member of the heron family',[95] has begun to over-winter here, and bearded tits have made an appearance. But it is not just birds that are to be found on Otmoor: butterflies emerge in profusion – some thirty species occur here – and at least eighteen species of dragonfly and damselfly skim over the ponds and ditches throughout the summer months.

The other innovative dimension in the planning and eventual construction of the motorway, really a progression from one aspect of the first, was the manner in which the Department of Transport took unprecedented steps to try and blend the motorway into its surroundings and to protect, even encourage, the diverse wildlife whose habitat had been disrupted. The Waterstock end of the motorway was the last section to be completed in 1991, and the bridge over the River Thame just one of forty-eight bridges that needed to be constructed between Waterstock and Birmingham.

Just past the motorway bridge, Holton Brook arrives from the north, having itself collected the waters of several other brooks and streams around Bernwood Forest, among them Danes Brook and Moorbridge Brook. The Thame, with its subsidiary mill stream, passes Holton Mill, sandwiched between the incessant rumble and roar of traffic from both the M40 motorway and the A40 trunk route that run almost parallel at this point, and almost unseen amongst its dense baffle of evergreens. First mention of a mill here is around 1279, with another reference in 1317. At one time the mill was owned by the Whorwoods, a family with links by birth and marriage to both John Hampden and Oliver Cromwell. The present building is of seventeenth-century origins, but now modernised. A neighbouring farm, closer to Wheatley, seems likewise marooned in the triangle formed of our ancient river, a medieval highway, and a modern dual carriageway, and we turn our attention now to the next section of the river beginning with one of its oldest crossings.

six

Wheatley to Chippinghurst

they procéed togither as one by ... Milton, Cuddesdo ...

When the new stretch of the A40 trunk road was built in 1963, bypassing the village of Wheatley and thereby relieving its people of the endless procession of traffic flowing between London and Oxford and the Midlands, the River Thame was once again something of a nuisance to the civil engineers, necessitating yet another bridge. Within a 100 yards or so of this point, one of the newer crossings, and again a rather unremarkable structure, the Thame flows under a bridge at the site of one of the oldest crossings over the river. Wheatley Bridge stands on one of the old highways of England, a strategic route indeed, for a little to the west of the crossing, the old main road from London forked; the left, via Shotover Hill and its commanding view of the city, on to Oxford and thence Gloucester; the right, via Islip, following the old Roman salt way to Worcester and the nearby salt mines at Droitwich.

In Roman times, Chester was the commercial centre for salt production in and around Cheshire, but it was later largely laid waste by the Normans, allowing Droitwich to emerge as the leading salt town. Droitwich, or *Salinae*, as it was known to the Romans, and *Hellath Wenn* to the Anglo-Saxons, had long been a key source of salt, a commodity of enormous importance in those early times, particularly because of its preservative properties. Such was its significance to the Romans that most Italian cities, including Rome, were founded near salt works. We take it for granted, perhaps even trivialise its significance (take it with a pinch of salt, even), and take for granted too its use in our language. Romans salted their green vegetables, believing this to counteract their natural bitterness, and eventually this led to our use of the word 'salad'. Salacious is from the Latin word *salax*, meaning 'a man in love', but literally 'in the salted state'. The Roman army paid its soldiers in salt, hence our word 'salary', and therefore 'to be worth your salt' was to earn your pay. Thus production and distribution of salt was a matter of high priority for the Romans and they developed a sophisticated network of roads emanating from Droitwich, with roads to the capital being of particular importance.

The road through Wheatley to London was clearly highly significant in commercial terms, therefore, but it was important also in terms of military strategy. The crossing, and later the bridge, has been a key location in struggles between opposing forces for hundreds of years, from the times of the inter-tribal conflicts of ancient Britain through to the skirmishes between King and Parliament during the Civil War,

Wheatley Bridge, from the eastern side.

during which period superiority and control of the crossing changed from side to side with some regularity. The river and bridge marked a strategic boundary between Parliament in London and the Crown at Oxford, and was crucial to the defence, or, depending on one's allegiance, blockade of Oxford, not to mention the road beyond from Oxford to Worcester. The bridge, or the road over it, was considered significant even at the time of the Second World War when the Home Guard blocked it with a telegraph pole and barbed wire, and this caution was perhaps justified, as the bridge was considered worthy of attack by enemy planes in October 1942.

It was the military factor that gave rise to the bridge's earlier names. At one time it was known as Harpesford or Herford Bridge, as it was then named after the ford that preceded it, recorded as early as AD 956. The Anglo-Saxon name *herpath*, from which these names are derived, was a commonly used term, and generally taken to signify a road made, or certainly sufficiently wide enough, for military purposes. The first record of a bridge, probably wooden, is from the twelfth century, when Henry II afforested land leading up to the crossing. There is record also of repairs to the bridge in 1286, when perhaps it was rebuilt in stone. Certainly by Leland's time, 'Whateley Bridge of 8 arches of stone is a 3 miles lower by water on Tame than Ikeford Bridge'.[96]

Later, there was a petition to Archbishop William Laud by the villagers of Milton and other neighbouring communities, complaining that Oxford carriers were ruining the bridge by carrying unreasonable loads of up to sixty tons each. Laud sent a request to the Chancellor of the University asking that not more than six horses to a cart be used. Laud, incidentally, opposed Puritanism and was suspected of Catholic sympathies, but became Archbishop of Canterbury from 1633-39. Prior to this tenure, and when he was Bishop of London and himself Chancellor of the University of Oxford, Laud was instrumental in establishing a Chair in Arabic at the University, primarily to accommodate a former pupil of Lord Williams's School, Edward Pocock (1604-91) who was making his mark in the academic world. Laud, incidentally, was also one of the four founders of the University Press at Oxford.

Pocock, later to become a renowned orientalist and ordained theologian, and, 'a scholar whose learning was the admiration of Europe',[97] was born in Oxford and received his early education at Thame School during the thirty-year headship of Richard Boucher, the golden period that generated so many other famous names. Pocock himself went on to Corpus Christi College, Oxford where he studied Oriental languages, and later, from 1630-1636, he became chaplain to the English 'Turkey Merchants' trading out of Aleppo in the Levant, before taking up Laud's new Chair of Arabic at Oxford in 1636. He spent the period from 1637-1640 in Constantinople, and on returning to England in 1647, (by which time Laud had been imprisoned in the Tower and executed), resumed his professorship of Arabic at Oxford. In 1649 he also became Professor of Hebrew, a position he held until his death. During his lengthy career, he wrote numerous biblical commentaries, as well as scholarly translations and works on Arabic history, and whilst in the East he amassed a superb collection of valuable manuscripts that is now housed in the Bodleian Library at Oxford.

A believer in the divine right of kings, Laud was a close ally of Charles I, and inevitably, perhaps, shortly after the King was beheaded, Laud was also executed in 1645, having been impeached for treason by the Long Parliament. Some would claim that his forceful views and alliance to Charles I contributed substantially to the political climate that gave rise to the Civil War. Ironically, fifteen years after his death and following the Restoration, Laud's own cortege travelled over Wheatley Bridge on its journey from All Hallows, Barking, in London, where he had been buried initially after his execution, to his final resting place in St John's College, Oxford.

Whatever the outcome of Laud's request to the Chancellor earlier in the century, wear and tear on the busy crossing point at Wheatley Bridge required that further repair and modification took place over subsequent centuries, considerably altering the appearance of the crossing. In 1642 the bridge and its approaches were about ten feet-wide, wide enough for two cavalrymen to ride abreast. There were eight pointed arches with pedestrian refuges above the cutwaters. A little way east of the main bridge was a ninth arch, Little Wheatley Bridge, which spanned a winter stream. A year later one of the arches was evidently broken and a gate and drawbridge installed. The bridge is mentioned by John Ogilby (1600-1676) in his innovative work *Britannia*, published in 1675. John Ogilby, the cartographer, should not be confused with John Ogilvie (1733-1813), the Scottish writer who published an epic poem, also called *Britannia*, in a work running to twenty volumes!

Ogilby's work is regarded as something of a watershed in the mapping of England and Wales. As well as, obviously, roads, his maps included notes on walls and hedges, bridges and fords, and even the method of cultivation of fields adjacent to the roads he described. Hills were drawn to indicate the direction and relative steepness of their incline. Ogilby focussed on the principal routes of his day, and as we have seen, the road over the Wheatley Bridge and River Thame was certainly a key highway. In 1809 there is a record of further rebuilding of Wheatley Bridge, using stone from nearby Holton quarry, forming three semi-circular arches with projecting keystones, and a single arch on each approach, whilst in 1820, the Stokenchurch and Wheatley Turnpike Trust funded the widening of 'the little bridge'. The oldest identified part of the existing structure is the 500-year-old (dry) arch embedded in the eastern end.

The evolution of this crossing point of the River Thame is typical of many, and so this is perhaps a suitable point to interrupt our own journey to briefly examine the general development of the bridge over many centuries. It has been claimed that 'ancient bridges are portals of history',[98] and the novelist John Buchan wrote that, 'history – social, economic, and military – clusters more heavily about bridges than about towns and citadels'.[99] The need, or even the simple desire to get to the other side of the river, has surely existed almost as long as man has been creating history, and the ability to do so without getting one's feet wet was doubtless a bonus. Thus whilst the earliest communities would have forded rivers at suitable points, (a practice that continued well beyond the time when man had the capability of building bridges), there has been a continual drive to find ways to walk, or ride, or drive over to the other bank. Materials lying close to hand would have been an obvious choice for those early engineers; boulders for stepping-stones; a fallen tree trunk to straddle the gap; or forest tendrils intertwined to form an elementary suspension bridge.

Clapper bridges, consisting of flat stone slabs supported on vertical boulder piers, doubtless have ancient origins, but continued to be made until relatively recent times. They are particularly common in the granite moors of the West Country, Exmoor's Tarr Steps, with its seventeen spans and primeval appearance, being an impressive example.

Bridge building in Britain is largely a legacy of the Romans, though their bridges were not as good as their roads, and their earliest wooden structures have not survived the passage of time, having rotted or been swept away by floods, or in some cases, burnt down. Timber, in fact, continued to be used for bridge building well into the railway era, so the Romans were not completely off-track with their choice of materials in this area. Bridges gradually replaced fords at strategic crossing places, though it was a slow process; of well over 600 river crossings mentioned in Anglo-Saxon charters, less than one fifth are bridges, the remainder being fords. At the time of the Domesday Book, over 450 settlements were named after fords, whereas there is virtually no mention of places named after bridges.

One of the Roman ideas that did survive was the packhorse bridge. This was a small, single-span, arched bridge, usually quite narrow and with low or non-existent parapets, so as not to jostle or damage the packs of merchandise suspended from either side of the horse's saddle. Though introduced in Roman times, most remaining examples of this type of bridge, on the whole to be found in the north of the country, date from the fourteenth century onwards. The Romans, meanwhile, continued to rely heavily on ferries to cross the major rivers. Not until medieval times did arched stone bridges seriously begin to emerge as reasonable alternatives to fords and ferries as far as the wider key crossings were concerned. In most cases, these medieval bridges had projecting piers, known as 'cutwaters', usually triangular in shape, with the point facing towards the stream to protect the pier from the force of the water and the impact of trees and other debris borne along by the water. Stone ribbing reinforced the undersides of the arches, and the upper parts of the piers often included recesses, or refuges, to enable pedestrians to evade a passing cart or horseman.

Generally, the shape of the arches reflected that used in church architecture and evolved accordingly. The earliest were semi-circular Norman arches, with barrel vaults. These gave way in the thirteenth century to narrower, pointed Gothic arches with groined vaults, and these in turn became more rounded again in the fifteenth century, and flatter still at the end of the medieval period. A typical medieval bridge was extremely long and would often include a substantial stone causeway that incorporated subsidiary floodwater arches, leading to the bridge across a floodplain; Folly Bridge in Oxford in the sixteenth century, for example, had a causeway with a remarkable forty-two arches.

It was not uncommon for other buildings to be associated with bridges; often a chapel would be built adjacent to, or even incorporated within the bridge, as a place where travellers could receive a blessing (and pay their tolls, of course), and Monmouth famously has a central gateway guarding the approaches to the town by way of a tower added to the thirteenth-century Monnow Bridge by Henry of Lancaster. The medieval, stone London Bridge, that replaced an earlier wooden Roman structure, was built over a period of more than thirty years either side of the end of the twelfth century, and included an array of well over 100 shops and houses. Prominent among these, though not added until 1577, was the flamboyant, timbered Nonsuch House, complete with its own chapel and Dutch-style gables. At its southern end, the bridge's gatehouse displayed the tar-preserved severed heads of various 'traitors', including William Wallace and Thomas More.

Almost exactly 600 years after work started on Old London Bridge, Abraham Darby III built in 1779–1781 the first iron bridge in Britain, spanning the Severn, but the subsequent rivalry between stone and iron as the material of choice for major bridges was effectively to end with the introduction of concrete at the beginning of the twentieth century. Dare one say that the charm of the bridge also ended? Fortunately, Wheatley Bridge still retains its ancient style, and even repairs necessary at the time of writing have been achieved without detriment to the character of this local landmark.

Just a few hundred yards downstream from Wheatley Bridge, past the Bridge Hotel and adjacent supermarket, the river, broader at this point, flows between the brick and stone abutments of the old GWR railway bridge. The Oxford (Cowley) to Princes Risborough branch line (via Thame), and therefore also the bridge, was opened in October 1864, and proved to be of particular value during the Second World War, when it was used by American military hospital trains. The line was poorly patronised in the post-war years and was closed in January 1963, when Dr Beeching axed the service as part of his infamous cost-cutting exercise in the early to mid-1960s. The bridge was demolished soon afterwards, just about 100 years after it was built. Not long before the demise of the line, *Evening Star*, the last steam locomotive to be constructed in Great Britain and earmarked for the museum from the moment it was built in Swindon in 1960, passed over the bridge on its historic commemorative journey around the country, shortly before it was withdrawn from service for preservation in 1965.

The village of Wheatley has developed a little way north-west of its bridges, and mostly around the little stream, now culverted, in a valley set at right angles to the Thame. Hills around the south-western side of the village rise quite sharply, but are not a significant deterrent to modern housing developers. Their counterparts in Roman times likewise built a villa on Castle Hill in Wheatley; unearthed in 1845, its existence is an indication of the significance of Wheatley as a Roman settlement, whilst the remains of a Saxon cemetery, discovered in 1883, confirm the antiquity of settlement here.

The village's quarry provided stone for constructions such as Windsor Castle and Oxford's Merton College, as well as other local cottages and ecclesiastical buildings. It also provided the venue for less illustrious activity: cock fighting and badger or bull baiting took place here, activities relished by quarrymen and local villagers alike, not to mention young well-to-dos from nearby Oxford. The rather unusual pyramidal stone lock-up, built in 1834 next to the parish pit, is perhaps a legacy of those boisterous times. It was used to lock up drunks and other miscreants overnight before being sent to the Oxford courts, a sobering prospect indeed, for with no windows and a floor space of only about six square feet plus stocks for added security and discomfort, the offenders doubtless regretted their excesses come morning.

The locality posed a greater threat than that derived from drunken quarrymen, however. Stagecoaches travelled through Wheatley and over the Thame *en route* to and from London, and the village was a convenient point at which to change horses. Not surprisingly, the descent from Shotover to Wheatley was a favourite haunt of 'freebooters' or highwaymen. The notorious Dick Turpin plied his trade in these parts for a time while based at nearby Appleford, and a year or so before Turpin was hanged for his ways, the preacher John Wesley was accosted by a highwayman near to Shotover in 1737. He gave up his purse, and the highwayman, trusting the word of a clergyman, let Wesley go on his way when told he had no money in his pockets, even though, according to the tale, this was not strictly true. Although there was presumably no convenient alternative or safer route, the threat of the highwaymen clearly did not deter important travellers. John Milton, with family links to this part of Oxfordshire (his grandfather was a forest ranger in the royal forest at Shotover), rode through Wheatley in 1642 to claim the hand of Mary Powell of Forest Hill Manor. The marriage was a troubled one, and Mary died ten years later, shortly after the birth of their third child. Even royalty came this way: Queen Elizabeth I travelled the route, both as a prisoner Princess and later as Queen in Progress, as did James I and Charles I.

Kings may come, and kings may go, but the Thame, like Tennyson's brook, just keeps going, and from Wheatley, the river maintains a broadly southwards course, all the while continuing its gentle convolutions and meanderings. It divides yet again at a sluice gate, just before the arrival of Cuddesdon Brook, the left-hand channel going over a weir with a drop of about three feet. The division necessitates two bridges when the river reaches Cuddesdon Mill, which is externally a rather austere, three-storey stone building. The Mill Bridge, across the loop of the river, is of stone, with a parapet wall and two unequal width arches and a single cutwater. The larger arch conveys water to the mill, the smaller, still bearing a remnant of its sluice gate mechanism, carries off excess water. Cuddesdon Bridge is rather larger: in 1874 it too had two arches, but by 1878 it had been enlarged with three wider arches either side of the two original ones, using stone from nearby Holton. It is built mostly of brick, the central arch having iron railings instead of a stone parapet. Close by is a DEFRA-funded wildflower conservation meadow, and a network of public or permissive footpaths.

The eighteenth-century watermill once belonged to Cuddesdon Manor, but even before that, Abingdon Abbey had a mill on this site that was lost in the course of the Viking invasions, though later recovered. In the Middle Ages, the millstream back as far as the weir was used as a fishery, belonging to the Mill. There was a minor altercation in 1066 when Peter, the new King William's representative, together with some of the Bishop of Lincoln's tenants at Great Milton, threatened to destroy the weir, but was thwarted by Abbot Ealdred, supposedly with the assistance of the miraculous powers of the bones of St Vincent. A contemporary account in the Abingdon Chronicle described how a storm and earthquake on one side of the river caused chaos amongst the Bishop's supporters, whilst those of the Abbot watched the debacle from the opposite bank.

Whether or not fishing rights was the issue at the heart of that particular dispute, signs near here now remind us of that normally more peaceful aspect of river life. It is said that more people are drawn to the banks of our rivers by angling than by any other activity, and indeed the status of angling as Britain's most popular participation sport can be traced back many years, and doubtless is in part a legacy of the Middle Ages when it was more of a necessity than a recreation.

Cuddesdon Mill and mill bridge.

Cuddesdon Bridge, its arches nearly occluded by the swollen river.

Anglers on the River Thame, 1989. (Photograph courtesy of *The Thame Gazette*)

Certainly from Winchendon and onwards downstream, the River Thame merits serious consideration as a location for the committed angling enthusiast. The waters are fished by flourishing local societies as well as those from more distant towns that have no river to call their own. They are fished by those content to engage in more solitary activity –'apart, silent, patient, unconcerned at the prospect of total failure'[100] – and play host to competitions and cups, claim and counterclaim, and inevitable tales of 'the one that got away'.

One of the delights of considering a river in its entirety is to observe the changes that occur from start to finish: physical changes that in turn determine the flora and fauna that the changing habitat will sustain. Fish, like those that do their utmost to land them, have their own likes and dislikes. Some prefer faster flowing, clearer waters: others murky, weed-infested waters. Some prefer a life near the surface, sometimes leaping for flying insects, other prefer to loiter in the depths, feeding along the bottom mud. There are some thirty-eight native species of fresh-water fish in British waters, and only about twelve or so that are of interest to anglers. Those known to fishermen on the Thame include dace, chub, bleak, gudgeon, bream, tench, roach, rudd, perch, barbel and pike – almost the full set.

We should perhaps mention the crayfish, which of course, is not a fish, but a ten-limbed crustacean, a relation of the lobster. Only one species is native to Britain, and the River Thame, like many others across the country, was once host to this species, the white-clawed crayfish *(Austropotamobius pallipes)*. Nowadays, the Thame is increasingly affected by infestation by non-native crayfish, the signal crayfish (*Pacifastacus leniusculus*) being the chief culprit. It was introduced into England and Wales in the late 1970s and early 1980s for farming purposes, but subsequently escaped from many of the sites into which it was introduced. It is quite capable of walking overland in search of a home, can rapidly colonise freshwater sites, and can not only competitively exclude our native crayfish, but also carries a fungal disease, the crayfish plague, to which the native crayfish has no defence. In addition to the potential impact on its fellow crayfish, signal crayfish have also been shown to have detrimental effects on other native fauna in British waters. Anglers find them a nuisance as they take their bait and burrow into riverbanks. All in all, not a popular addition to our rivers.

Away from the river itself, Cuddesdon stands half a mile away at the top of a steepish hill to the right (west) of the river. It commands good views across the plain of Oxford, the Thame valley and away to the Chiltern Hills that, like, 'Hounds of Heaven ... keep immemorial vigil over the Vale'[101] from as far upstream as Aylesbury. Bishops of Oxford resided at Cuddesdon for several centuries in the Old Palace, a property acquired through the munificence of John Fell whom we mentioned earlier. The grand old house was burned down in 1960, though not for the first time in its history, for during the Civil War the original house, built by John Bancroft, the seventh Bishop of Oxford, using timber from Shotover and Stow Wood, was deliberately fired by the Governor of Oxford to prevent Parliamentary troops from using it. Nearby is the theological training establishment now known as Ripon College, founded over 100 years ago by Bishop 'Soapy Sam' Wilberforce, as Cuddesdon College. During the Second World War the college was temporarily taken over by the government for a rather different purpose; it was used as a hostel for some of the Irish girls who worked in the nearby Cowley factories.

The principal of the college is also vicar of the parish and over the years most of those who have held this post later became bishops – notable among them the former Archbishop of Canterbury, Dr Robert Runcie, who was principal for most of the 1960s. An aside of ecclesiastical interest is that *Cuddesdon* is the name of a well-known tune to words of the hymn *At the Name of Jesus*. It was composed by the Revd Canon William Harold Ferguson (1874-1950), a musician and clergyman who spent most of his adult life working in prestigious public schools. Another of his tunes is *Wolvercote*, the name of a village just to the north of Oxford. Use of these names implies that the writer had some local knowledge, and Ferguson was indeed warden of nearby Radley College for some twelve years from 1925.

Where there is water there will sadly be accidents, and the River Thame has not been immune to its share of tragedy, as we have already mentioned. Another such event occurred in the midsummer of 1902, at a time of heavy flooding in the Oxford area. A lecturer from Cuddesdon College took a group of choirboys to bathe in the river. Things went well until the strong current carried one of the boys away. The lecturer, who was also curate of Cuddesdon parish and said to be a good swimmer, went to his assistance, but sadly both he and the boy were drowned. Their bodies were recovered some distance downstream several hours later.

Like several other towns and villages across the country, including Haddenham and Long Crendon, Cuddesdon has its own mummer play. It dates back to at least 1914, thus perpetuating what is surely one of the most curious traditions in the land. Mummer plays are usually performed at Christmas time, but in certain regions at Halloween, All Souls' Day, New Year, Plough Monday or Easter, by a group of men usually with blackened faces and dressed in tatter coats.

Each town's mummer play would be slightly different to everyone else's – perhaps some famous (or infamous) local figure would be depicted. Although the scripts vary throughout the country they mostly follow the same basic theme: a hero (often Saint/King George) and villain fight and one of them is killed; a doctor is called and the dead man is miraculously revived. There is often an element of comedy and the scene usually ends with a seasonal song. It may be that these plays are a ritual commemoration of the death of the old year and the birth of the new. Other themes give rise to Recruiting Sergeant, Wooing, and Sword Dance plays. The scripts are usually only a few minutes long, written as doggerel rather than poetry, and typically are performed by villagers going from house to house or pub to pub. The tradition has largely died out but dedicated folklore enthusiasts still maintain the custom.

But we should return to the river. Shortly past Cuddesdon Mill and the two bridges, the millstream rejoins the main river, and the land rises quite sharply on the left hand side, where a motorcycle scramble track recently scarred the fields. The river curves to the west and then southwards, whereupon it is crossed by a power line, and around the next bend, Chippinghurst Manor comes into view.

Chippinghurst is a tiny hamlet set on a knoll in a valley south of Denton. It has a history that can be traced back to tenth-century Saxon beginnings: a medieval settlement here was mentioned in the Domesday Book, but no trace of that now remains. The place name means 'hill of Cibba' and the hamlet has been known previously as Chibnes(s), Chibbinghurst, Chibbenhurst and more recently, Chippenhurst. It now comprises little more than its Tudor manor house and a relatively modern dower house that was used as a maternity home in the Second World War. The Manor House was one of a number of Royal hunting lodges and was often visited by Henry II. The present building was probably built around the late sixteenth century.

The grounds of the Manor have for a number of years been the venue for an annual charity cricket match for the WellBeing charity for women and babies, an event supported by a host of sporting and show biz celebrities, such as Gary Lineker, Shane Warne and Mike Atherton, Carol Vorderman and David Frost. Other fund-raising matches involving teams from the Lords' Taverners also take place, again of course with the accompaniment of the rich and famous. The cricket field effectively has the river as one of its boundaries and seems almost as well cared for as the sacred turf of Lord's itself. On slightly higher ground, away from the river and towards the house, is a floodlit-tennis court for those of a different sporting inclination. The house itself was used by the English Football Association as the venue for preliminary interviews for the position of chief coach of the national side, shortly before the World Cup of 2006. As things transpired, the exercise proved fruitless, as the then favoured candidate, former Brazil and current Portugal manager Luis Felipe Scolari, turned down the FA's offer.

Chippinghurst Manor is a remote spot, accessible only from Denton Lane (the Cuddesdon to Chiselhampton road) or theoretically by footpath from Little Milton via stepping stones a little further down the river, when the water level is sufficiently low, of course. Five footpaths meet at this point by the river, and the stepping stones, which replaced a bridge, disappeared in the 1970s, causing local ramblers to engage in a long struggle with the county council to reinstate a crossing. At the time of writing, the matter was still unresolved, and the few stones that remain in place scarcely constitute a safe or suitable crossing point for 'professional' walkers, let alone casual Sunday afternoon strollers.

Shortly past this point, Haseley Brook joins from the eastern side, having itself passed under Hangman's Bridge (a seemingly popular name for bridges for the Thame's feeder streams) on the A329 road from Milton Common to Stadhampton. A little further on, to the western side of the river on Richmond Hill, is Great Copse, a large wooded area of at one time some twenty-three acres, originally planted in 1694 by John Doyley, and which apparently boasted the largest rookery in the British Isles. The Doyley family name crops up with some regularity in this part of the world, as we shall see from time to time. The name is commemorated in Doyleys Farm House, for example, reckoned to be the oldest building in Stadhampton, just a mile or so from Chiselhampton, a village we will visit shortly. Leland, who had earlier (from 1542-1552) been Rector of another nearby village, Great Haseley, recorded in around 1600 that land in these parts was 'fruitful of corn and grass, but barren of wood'.[102] He would doubtless have appreciated the change, had he made a return visit 100 years on. Great Copse has its roots in an age more than seventy years before the construction of the next major building to engage our attention, discovered as the river approaches a small village with perhaps disproportionate significance, for John Hampden at least.

seven

Chiselhampton to Drayton St Leonard

by … Chiselton. From hence our streame of Thame runneth to Newenton, Draton …

Chiselhampton House is built on a gravel terrace above the flood plain of the river. It is a tall, narrow, but imposing house built in distinctive red brick, locally made, with stone quoins. A porch with ionic pillars with the Peers' coat of arms in a cartouche was added at a later date. The house was rebuilt in 1766-68 for Charles Peers, son of a former Lord Mayor of London, and it was a London builder, Samuel Dowbiggin, who constructed the main building. Later, in 1820, an orangery was added, a five-sided glass structure with an umbrella-shaped roof. Previously, when it was known as Chiselhampton Manor, the property was owned by the Doyley family, who in all probability were descendents of Robert d'Oyley (alternatively d'Oilgi, D'Oilly, Doilie, or Doyley) of Lisieux, who had himself come to England at the time of the Norman Conquest, and was highly favoured by King William. Between 1067 and 1071, Robert, 'so powerful a man in his time, that no one durst oppose him',[103] built a fortified motte and bailey castle at Wallingford, where he also established the Benedictine Priory. He was later appointed Sheriff of Oxford, where he strengthened the city walls, probably constructed Grandpont, one of the main crossings over the Thames into Oxford from the south, built Oxford Castle, of which the tower remains to this day, and was given significant estates across Buckinghamshire, Oxfordshire and Gloucestershire, including Waterperry Manor, which was 'sublet' to the FitzElys family, whom we mentioned earlier. There is a remarkable alabaster memorial to other members of the D'Oyley family in St Mary's church in Hambleden; it commemorates Sir Cope D'Oyley, who died in 1633, his wife and their ten children. Some of the latter little figures are depicted carrying skulls, signifying that they predeceased their parents.

The River Thame runs past the grounds of the Chiselhampton House, behind which is the small Georgian church of St Katherine. The latter was rebuilt by Charles Peers in 1762, and has remained largely unrestored since then. One of its most distinctive features is the bell and clock turret at the western end, its clock face painted pale blue and for a while frozen in time at 5.35. The turret is an ornate construction, not unlike those found on stable blocks of the period, and seemingly rather top-heavy in comparison to the stuccoed building beneath. Inside the church, a panelled Jacobean oak pulpit is enclosed within the clerk's desk and surrounded by several manorial box pews. It has a tiny white marble font set on a wooden stem, and glass and other memorials to the Peers family.

The church now resides under the jurisdiction of the Redundant Churches Commission, in spite of the best efforts of those who tried their hardest to maintain its viability. One of these was the Poet Laureate John Betjeman, who, having a love of church architecture, championed endangered buildings and penned his own verses in tribute to this unique little building. *Verses Turned in aid of A Public Subscription towards the Restoration of the Church of St Katherine, Chiselhampton, Oxon* (1952) portrays in typical Betjeman style an evocative insight into the centrality of the church to village life in days gone by.

The church at Chiselhampton would not please everyone, needless to say. Augustus Welby Pugin (1812-1852) is regarded by some as the foremost British architect of the nineteenth century. He experienced a spiritual conversion to Catholicism that left him filled with a fervent desire to express his faith through architecture. He was particularly concerned about the lack of spirituality, and what he thought of as paganism, in the design of more recent churches, something he described as 'a Decay of Taste'.[104] Pugin likened these buildings to theatres, such that the focus of attention was the clergyman rather than the altar, and claimed that going to church in them was more of a social than a spiritual occasion. St Katherine's is a surviving example – having, 'pews that faced the pulpit, and a rail added around the altar simply to keep the dogs out'.[105] The latter is an oblique critical reference to a legacy of Archbishop Laud, who we mentioned earlier, who advocated a range of communion rails so designed as not to allow dogs to enter the sanctuary.

After the River Thame has left the house and church behind, it turns briefly to the west, where it is crossed by the Oxford to Stadhampton road. This is the only major crossing point of the river between Wheatley and Dorchester and thus has long been of considerable strategic importance, not least in the Civil War, for example. On one notable occasion that we have already mentioned, the bridge was manned by the Royalists to secure the retreat of Prince Rupert to Oxford after the Battle of Chalgrove Field in June 1643 at which John Hampden was fatally wounded. At this time, the bridge had gates, restricting the passage of pedestrians and horses to 'market days and sometimes in the daytime'.[106] Rupert had set out from Oxford on the evening of 17 June 1643 with the intention of hi-jacking a Parliamentarian pay wagon near Chinnor, and the following day crossed Chiselhampton Bridge with 1,700-1,800 men. On his return, in retreat, having failed in his principal objective, he sent some of his men ahead to secure the bridge and ambush the chasing Parliamentarians, but before the ambush could be set up, the Parliamentarian horse had caught up with Rupert and he turned to face his enemy in that now famous cornfield at Chalgrove. Hampden was the principal casualty of the rout that followed.

The significance of Chiselhampton as a crossing point of the Thame goes back considerably further than the Civil War, however, and there is mention of a Cheselhampton Brygwey in 1398 when it was reported that the King's road there was flooded, and not long after, pontage rights were granted in 1444. From

John Hampden memorial, Chalgrove.

the eighth century, Mercian kings had imposed 'three common dues', sometimes referred to as 'common obligations' or 'common burdens'. One of these was to fund bridge building, another to fund work on fortifications, and the third to provide men for military service (a precursor of conscription). Later, and for several centuries from the Middle Ages onwards, a number of additional tolls was applied in order to defray the costs of upkeep of, for example, town or city walls (known as murage) or streets (pavage). The principle and practice of pontage, a means of spreading the repair costs of a bridge among the townships on either side of the bridge and other travellers that used the bridge, likewise became the norm.

A stone bridge at Chiselhampton dates at least from the sixteenth century and John Leland described, 'five great pillars of stone, apon the which was laid a timbre bridge'.[107] In 1628 it was apparently called Doyley Bridge, presumably in honour of one of 'Great Copse' Doyley's forebears, perhaps even Robert d'Oyley himself. Soon after the Battle of Chalgrove, the bridge was broken down, to be repaired later in 1690. The present structure, some 178 feet-long and built of Headington stone, consists of eight low segmental arches and five stone pillars. Those on the south side are original; the northern side was widened by some eight feet in 1899 by means of iron girders on stone piers. The southern face has massive cutwaters, five of which have recesses for pedestrians. Just a little way to the south is a subsidiary single arch bridge over Cuxham Brook, which joins the Thame soon after, having made its way from Chalgrove and Stadhampton.

The village was originally called Hampton, a place name meaning 'high enclosure'. The prefix was added to indicate the nature of the gravel terrace upon which the village had developed (Old English *ceosol* or *cisel* = gravel or shingle), and to distinguish it from Brookhampton, just down the road, which also was originally called Hampton. In the south-west of the village, just a few hundred yards from the bridge, is Camoys (or Camoise) Court Farm, where the remains of a fourteenth-century farmhouse are incorporated into the present building, and where the remnant of an ancient moat can be seen, once protecting the farmhouse from the seasonal floodwaters of the nearby river. The property was owned by Sir Richard de Couches of Great Milton and later came into the possession of Sir Thomas de Camoys, hero and commander of the British left wing at the Battle of Agincourt.

Sir Thomas de Camoys, *c.* 1351-1421, was born and died in the Sussex village of Trotton, where there remain two visible reminders of his life. The first is a splendid brass, actually dated 1419 and 'signed' by the engraver, or at least his guild; the brass is claimed to be one of the most magnificent in England, and shows Lord Camoys, wearing the Order of the Garter, with his wife and son. Nearby, incidentally, is the (1310) brass of Margaret Camoys, from an earlier generation of the family, the first brass of a woman anywhere. The second reminder of Sir Thomas is the nearby ancient bridge over the Rother, built by him in around 1400. That it is constructed of stone is, as we have noted, quite unusual for the period.

A riverside walk from the main road near Chiselhampton Bridge towards Camoys Court Farm makes its way through a coppice of mostly young trees – oak, rowan

Chiselhampton Bridge, 1904. (Copyright photograph, reproduced by kind permission of Oxfordshire County Council Photographic Archive)

and alder among others – through which tantalising glimpses of the river may be seen. The delicate lemon-yellow undersides of grey wagtail, strutting at water's edge, complement the brilliant tones of the yellow water lily – 'brandy bottle' as some would call it – that grows in profusion here. In summer, damselflies, most noticeably the common coenagrion, abound here as elsewhere alongside the river, cavorting and flirting in flight, then settling in characteristic tandem mating position, their striking azure bodies gleaming in the sunlight, offering a conspicuous target for hungry wagtails and others.

From Chiselhampton, the river runs due south, picking up another little brook arising near the Baldons. This stream actually starts life closer to the Thames than the Thame, but the contour of the land favours the latter as its destination. At Chiselhampton, the Thame is only about four miles from the Thames, for crows at least, but each river flows rather more than that before their union, especially the Thames, whose convoluted path travels about three times further than that of the Thame to reach their mutual meeting point. For now, the Thame veers temporarily west, seemingly to avoid nearby Stadhampton, though the reality is doubtless that Stadhampton's earliest settlers chose the slightly higher ground away from the river and its seasonal floods. The main road out of Stadhampton, the A329 to Warborough, though set a little higher than the immediate water meadows, picks up the course of the river as for a mile or so it turns south-eastward, and seemingly away from its eventual destination. The river here is intermittently congested with dense masses of reeds and rushes; mallards and warblers, not to mention the ubiquitous banded damselflies are among their residents. Winter flocks of harsh-chuckling fieldfare swarm from tree to tree, whilst venturesome red kites maintain a soaring surveillance some distance from their favoured nesting grounds further east.

The hamlet of Great Holcombe is scarcely conspicuous from the road and Newington, likewise, is quickly passed; yet Newington's few buildings are sufficiently striking as to make their mark on passing travellers.

Two significant buildings lie close to the river here, as it curves round almost ninety degrees *en route* to Drayton St Leonard. By some quirk of ecclesiastical organisation, the little church of St Glen remained under the direct jurisdiction of Canterbury until the nineteenth century. Like several of those we have visited on our convoluted journey, it has been much modified over the course of its existence, but has actually changed little now for several hundred years. Sheep graze nonchalantly in the churchyard, and perhaps have done so for several centuries. Inside the church there are Norman archways, and the font, with its Jacobean fretwork cover, dates from about 1200. The chancel timbers and screen date from the fifteenth century and thus are somewhat younger than the attractive octagonal spire with its sanctus bell that dates from 200 years earlier. In the church tower there is a more unusual relic, for a church at least: a canon ball, reputedly Parliamentarian, and fired during the Civil War. It evidently struck the church but without causing any significant damage.

Inside a recess in the chancel is the tomb of the last man to carry out major restoration of the church, some 600 or so years ago, and facing this is another rather curious monument. It commemorates Walter Dunch, who died in 1644, and his wife: they are depicted wrapped in shrouds that are tied under their chins and then in topknots over their heads. The Dunch family were rather influential in Oxfordshire and Berkshire over a number of generations around this period of history, being related by marriage to Cromwell; Members of Parliament; Sheriffs of Oxfordshire and so on. The family was not always entirely popular or successful, however. It was said of Edmund Dunch III that he, 'was the husband of the fine Mrs. Dunch; was a great favourite with the Protector, and had a patent to be lord of the Lord knows what, and how little he deserves it'.[108] His grandson, Edmund Dunch IV, is said to have lost the Wittenham estates to King James at cards, though the estates were returned on the condition that he never play again. Little Wittenham church, curiously, retains in its fourteenth-century tower, the 'Ace of Spades' window that local legend insists shows how playing cards enabled a local merchant to win the money to build it. Edmund, incidentally, was the last in the family line, dying in 1719 without male heir. One of his forebears, William Dunch, is commemorated in Little Wittenham church: his tomb was erected while he was still alive (a relatively common practice in the Middle Ages) but strangely the date of his death was never added. Other members of the Dunch family are commemorated in the church, including the nine- month-old daughter of Henry Dunch.

Next door to Newington church is Newington House, built around 1660 just a few years after the Civil War. It was built for Squire Dunch by one R. Frogley, and is a rather plain, albeit well proportioned building in grey stone. It somehow assumes a rather more stately appearance when viewed through wrought iron gates, hung from gate piers ornamented atop by shields and griffins that survey all those that pass by. The piers are recessed, like sentry boxes, giving an impression that busby-topped guards should really be standing within, impassively carrying out their token duty.

Beauforest House, formerly the rectory, and adjacent to the church on the Stadhampton side, is the only other building of note in Newington, but scarcely visible from the road. Built towards the end of the eighteenth century, part of the structure at the rear incorporates ceiling beams from an earlier rectory, possibly dating back to 1500.

At Newington, the River Thame begins the overall south-westward course that it will maintain until it finally reaches the Thames, though characteristically, there are still many twists and turns to come. Shortly after this point, and about two miles upstream from Dorchester, the river passes to the south-east side of another little Oxfordshire village, Drayton St Leonard.

There has been a settlement here since medieval times, yet the population of the village still numbers only a few hundred. All the more remarkable then, that Martha, a great-great-granddaughter of one Bartholomew Dandridge, born in Drayton St Leonard in around 1580, should later become, as Mrs George Washington, the First Lady of the United States of America. Her marriage in 1759 to the future President probably took place at the bride's plantation house in Virginia, aptly named 'The White House', inherited from her late first husband, a wealthy landowner named Daniel Parke Custis. It is said that behind every great man, there stands a great woman, but we are unlikely to know the full extent of Martha's influence in shaping what is now the most powerful nation on earth, for when George Washington died in 1799, Martha assured the lasting confidentiality of her personal life by burning their private letters.

Doubtless the fact that the Thame can be forded at Drayton St Leonard was one of the reasons why a settlement was established well before Washington's forebears set off on their epic voyage of discovery to the New World in 1620. The ford is tucked away in a corner of the village that looks as though it has changed little for hundreds of years. It is rarely used by motor vehicles nowadays, though a procession of vintage tractors maintains the tradition in the course of an occasional Easter parade through South Oxfordshire. It is interesting that in some old documents there are references to deliveries to the village being made by river, and landing stages are shown on old maps, an indication that in spite of Taylor's rather derogatory comments quoted earlier, the Thame was once commercially navigable this far back from Dorchester. For recreational purposes, the river is of course navigable much further upstream as well as downstream, and kayaks and rowing boats, not to mention more makeshift pontoons and rafts, are occasionally to be seen along much of the river's length.

As elsewhere, the river at Drayton St Leonard is exceedingly prone to flooding, with very marked changes in both the level and the character of the river, for at such times it becomes much faster flowing. Even in extreme flooding, few of the local properties are adversely affected, but access to the village from Stadhampton to the north, via Hayward's Bridge over the Thame just south of Stadhampton, can be severely restricted. Consequently, at some stage during most winters, the only other vehicular access on a metalled road is from Berinsfield, to the west of the village. The crossing at Hayward's Bridge used to be a ford: a footbridge is shown on a map dated 1841, and the road bridge was built in 1884, funded by public subscription, and erected, according to a tablet on the bridge, to the memory of one Frank Aldworth, by his labourers. Raised walkways extend for some way along the Berinsfield Road, a constant reminder of the vulnerability of the area to flooding. From this point on, the contrasting ancient and modern features of Wittenham Clumps and Didcot's cooling towers come regularly to view.

Drayton St Leonard itself has a mix of buildings from several centuries. The little church of St Catherine and St Leonard, built mostly of stone, but now pebble-dashed, is likewise a typical blend of features accrued over hundreds of years. The nave is Norman, the chancel, with its floor of yellow tiles, mostly fourteenth century. The free-standing oak-shingled bell tower, supported by a framework of heavy oak and chestnut timbers and rising up through the roof, is thought to be older than much of the main part of the church. The church, like Newington, which was a 'peculiar' of Canterbury, and Thame, a 'peculiar' of Lincoln, was, along with those at nearby Warborough and Little Wittenham, one of the twelve Dorchester 'peculiars' that, until the suppression, came under the jurisdiction of one other than the bishop of the diocese, in this case the Abbot of Dorchester Abbey church, rather than the Bishop of Dorchester.

The church is by no means the only old building in the village: two delightful Elizabethan cottages, timbered and thatched, stand close to the ford across the Thame. Drayton House, at the southernmost point of the village, is a timber-framed building with brick infilling in a herringbone pattern, and behind Drayton House is a splendid barn, adjudged by some to be the finest building in the village. Sometimes known as Haseley Barn or the Tithe Barn, it is a timber framed, weather-boarded building of six bays with a massive hipped and tiled roof, and dates from no later than the fifteenth century.

A short distance past Drayton St Leonard, as the river turns briefly due west, it passes under a footbridge, an arched, rusted metal structure with wooden planking, and soon the river flows past an area where once there were osiers, or willow beds. Willows are very much part of the country landscape, found typically by rivers, streams and ditches, and over the thirty or so miles of the course of the Thame so far, numerous willows can be seen growing near its banks. Some are pollarded, some grow freely, some are upright, intact; many are arched, split and twisted. The common species in these situations, *Salix fragilis* or crack willow, thrives in the wet meadows

Flooded ford, Drayton St Leonard.

of the Thame, oblivious to the temporary flooding to which they are victim. Not surprisingly, the willow has had an important and varied place in rural life, with almost as many uses as there are species and varieties: poles for fencing; withies for basket making; hurdles; sieves; milk pails, even beehives. The bark was used for tanning, the roots for dyeing; the list goes on. In more recent times, wood from the Essex white willow has been used in the making of cricket bats, whilst that from the Bedford willow was once used in the production of artificial wooden legs. Such was the importance of this wood in medieval times that each district would have its own osier beds, most commonly planted with the green or purple stemmed varieties, particularly the common osier, *Salix viminalis*, for cropping and pollarding. Now, for Drayton St Leonard, such facilities are essentially a thing of the past, remembered only by an evocative street name, the lesser commercial demand for willow products being fulfilled by such places as Sedgemoor in the Somerset levels.

eight

Queenford to Dorchester

by … Dorchester (sometime a bishops see, and a noble citie) and so into the Thames …

The final few miles of the Thame after it has left Drayton St Leonard consists of a series of exaggerated twists and bends, the river seemingly snaking and turning in a final effort to somehow resist its inevitable destiny. At the start of these contortions, the river divides once again at a weir, with a small drop to the left-hand channel. The main river takes the slightly longer right-hand course, and soon turns again, past the first of a number of old gravel pits, now variously used for contrasting activities – the swirl and whine of jet-skis in one, the unhurried peace and tranquillity of the angler in another. Water is a great attraction to many birds, whether water fowl or not, and the Dorchester pits have consequently become a popular spot for birdwatchers, with a wide range of both resident and transient birds on view (jet-skiers permitting, of course).

Tucked in here between gravel pits on one side and the river, its two arms once more reunited, on the other, is Queenford Farm. On a little side stream there was a watermill here in medieval times – a mill is mentioned in the Domesday Book, and Queenford Mill is mentioned by name in documents from 1146. It was leased to a succession of the local wealthy, including Richard Beauforest and William Dunch, familiar names to readers of our story. The present building, of eighteenth-century origins, is partly brick and partly timber-framed and weather-boarded, and was in use as a mill until the end of the nineteenth century.

Another curve of the river takes it south-east towards Warborough, before it turns back through ninety degrees, and so under the modern Dorchester bypass and the constant thunder of traffic travelling along the busy road between Oxford and Henley and beyond. The bridge, built in 1982, has three sections, named from north to south, Monk's Bridge, Abbey Bridge (over the main river) and Priest's Moor Bridge. It is disappointingly a rather monotonous structure, the smooth concrete under-surfaces of its arches an inevitable target for local graffitists, most conspicuously one named Jimmy.

When just through the bridge, the river divides yet again at a weir, the right hand channel dropping three feet or so into Buck Pool, before embarking on a long curve round to Dorchester Abbey. The left hand stream, Overy Mill Race, takes the rather more direct route to the point at which the two channels merge again, just north of the old Henley Road into the village of Dorchester.

Overy Mill. (Photograph by Henry Taunt, 1870, reproduced by kind permission of English Heritage NMR)

In between these two arms of the river, effectively on an island, is Hurst Water Meadow, recently developed as a pleasant little nature reserve. Access to the meadow is via a narrow footbridge close to Overy Mill and over its stream, or by means of Long Bridge, a single-span steel-girder bridge installed in 1998 after an earlier structure, a concrete deck on wooden piers, collapsed a year or so previously. The meadow is likely to have been an integral part of the Overy Mill water system from as far back as the eighth century. A pasture described as 'Le Hurst' was mentioned in some fourteenth-century records, and seems to have changed ownership a number of times over the intervening centuries until in 1996 it was purchased from the receiver on behalf of a trust funded by public subscription. One of the principal objectives of the trust was to preserve and conserve this ancient meadow, together with its wildlife and their habitats, whilst at the same time retaining for the public a safe and enjoyable recreational facility. From time immemorial, children (and their parents) have used the meadow for bathing and fishing, and such pursuits seem assured at least for several more generations.

Buck Pool, a surprisingly deep pool at the eastern end of the meadow and not recommended for swimming, takes its name from a seventeenth-century Oxfordshire word for a basket used to catch eels, or the frame supporting a basket attached to a sluice. The meadow seems to engender colloquial vocabulary: locals talk of the Scrape (a man-made depression in an already low-lying part of the meadow, in which to retain water after heavy rain or flooding, so adding to the biodiversity of the meadow), the Slips (a long, narrow strip of the meadow that once was itself a separate island, bounded by the Thame to the north and the 'rushing stream' to the south), and the Bunds (small dams across the old drain that was once a 'rushing stream'). Buck Pool is overlooked by a black poplar that has recently been somewhat disfigured by radical surgery to render it safe to passers-by. Osiers are here too, and some of the river banks have been protected by willow 'spiling', a process whereby live willow stakes, which have the potential to create root systems with ease, are driven into the base of the bank, a wattle made by weaving osier withies, and the ensuing structure lined with hessian and back-filled with earth.

Overy Mill, probably dating back to the eighth century and mentioned, like Queenford, in the Domesday Book, was originally part of the Dorchester Abbey estate, passing to private ownership after the Dissolution in 1536. It remained working until the early twentieth century, but now is badly in need of restoration.

Our journey along the Thame has finally brought us to the village of Dorchester itself, perhaps one of the most historic places in southern England, certainly in the context of church history, for the town, described as 'the cradle of English Christianity',[109] is famed for its contribution to the growth and spread of Christianity over much of England. It was at Dorchester in AD 635 that St Birinus, a missionary bishop sent from Rome, baptised Cynegils, King of the West Saxons, in the River Thame. Indeed, not only Cynegils, but according to the Venerable Bede, his Witan (council) were also baptised. The cynic might read a political motive into the event. The occasion was sponsored by King Oswald of Northumbria, and it strengthened the alliance of those who had adopted the new Christian faith against King Penda, the last remaining pagan ruler. If that was not enough, King Oswald was wishing to marry Cynegils' daughter, and was perhaps keen to foster good pre-marital relations!

St Birinus, the 'Apostle of Wessex', established a See at Dorchester and built there his first cathedral on land given him by the two kings. Within little more than 200 years, Dorchester had become the centre of the large Mercian diocese, which extended from the Thames right up to the River Humber. Nothing now remains of this original Saxon cathedral, for not long after he established himself in Britain, William the Conqueror moved the centre of the See to Lincoln, installing Remigius as Bishop, and leaving Dorchester with an abbey, founded by Bishop Alexander around 1140 for a community of Augustinian canons, and built on the site of the old cathedral.

Without the impetus and status derived from being a cathedral city, Dorchester's significance diminished. Whatever charm twenty-first-century visitors and tourists may find, Camden in the late sixteenth century described the village as, 'weakened and impoverish'd, ... a mean and inconsiderable place' which 'sensibly began to decay'[110] after the exodus of the See. Dorchester has remained little more than a village to this day, and one writer has suggested that it, 'seems far too little for its history, like a boy wearing the clothes of a tall man'.[111] Writer Jerome K. Jerome (1859-1927), himself no stranger to the village, took a rather more pragmatic view, 'Dorchester is a delightfully peaceful old place, nestling in stillness and silence and

Buck Pool, Overy. (Photograph by kind permission of the Hurst Water Meadow Trust)

drowsiness. It is very old, and it was very strong and great once. Now it sits aside from the stirring world, and nods and dreams'.[112]

Jerome supposedly wrote at least some of his most famous work, *Three Men in a Boat*, from which these words are taken, while staying at the Barley Moe in nearby Long Wittenham in the late 1880s.

At the time of the Dissolution in 1536, much of the abbey was destroyed, but the Abbey church of St Peter and St Paul was purchased intact (for £140 – the value of the lead on the roof!) by wealthy local benefactor, Sir Richard Beauforest, (or Bewforest or Bewfforeste) who later bequeathed the church to the parish:

> Being 'sicke in bodye, and hole in mynde and memory (thanks be to God), considering nothing is more certen to men than death, and nothing more uncertain than the hour of death' he bequeathed the 'Abbey Churche of Dorchester .... to the Paryshe of Dorchester aforesaid, so that the said parishioners shall not sell, alter, or alienate the saide Churche, Implements, or any part or pell. thereof without the consent of my heirs or executors.[113]

It is a quite remarkable inheritance. The original Norman church was small, but was extended over succeeding centuries, with substantial restorations in 1970, such that it is now one of the most striking buildings in the Thames region.

Viewed from a distance in its setting close to the River Thame, the Abbey church dominates the more southerly aspect of the village, its long, almost barn-like roof

Black poplar. (Photograph by kind permission of the Hurst Water Meadow Trust)

and rather squat, square tower clearly visible from some way off. This simple, though striking exterior in no way prepares the visitor for what lies within.

A sixteenth-century entrance porch, surrounding very much older doors, leads into the People's chapel, once reserved for villagers' services. A blank wall momentarily obscures the grandeur to come. Blank, that is, except for the remnants of a once glorious fourteenth-century fresco, depicting the Crucifixion of Christ, with Mary and John turning away from the awful scene. In the People's chapel is a lead Norman font, one of only a few remaining in England, and the only one belonging to a monastic church to survive the Reformation. Lead was used for fonts, albeit rarely, to preclude seepage of the precious holy water through the stone that would ordinarily be used.

Given the number of lead fonts remaining in the country – some three dozen or so – it is all the more remarkable that three should be found so close together in this little corner of Oxfordshire; one here at Dorchester, another at St Laurence's at Warborough, a mile to the east of Dorchester, and the third, embossed with the figures of thirty archbishops, at St Mary's church in Long Wittenham, just two miles to the west of Dorchester. During the Civil War, the local churchwardens at Wittenham were so concerned that Cromwell's troops might melt down the font to provide lead for making bullets, they encased their twelfth-century treasure in wood, and it remained thus hidden for almost 200 years! The unusually large lead font in the twelfth-century flint-walled Pilgrim church at Pyecombe in West Sussex, a village where for generations, shepherds' crooks were wrought by the village blacksmiths from gun barrels as well as other more conventional materials, was disguised for the same reason, in this instance by a liberal application of whitewash, traces of which are said to remain to this day.

A brief whistle-stop tour of lead fonts around the country would surely make mention of the circular font at St Augustine's church at Brookland, on Romney Marsh, that is thought to have been fashioned by Norman or Flemish craftsmen in the twelfth century. Quite how it came to be at Brookland is less certain; perhaps some of the smugglers, so active in that remote area over many centuries, or a group of sailors on one of their raids to the French coast, could offer an explanation. St Augustine's, alongside the famous octagonal wooden belfry with its conical roof of three diminishing 'flounces' that stands apart from the church, was built on a small mound to lift it above the flood-water level of the Marsh, a ploy reminiscent of similar action in villages along the Thame in our own story. The font itself is decorated with occupations relating to each month of the year, and, unusually, with the signs of the Zodiac, a curious throwback to paganism. The font at Dorchester is more 'ec' (ecclesiastically correct)! It is beautifully crafted, with eleven arches around its side, each one revealing the figure of an Apostle (presumably no space for Judas). Some consider that one of the figures actually represents Jesus. That being the case, which other apostle is missing? Perhaps sceptical Thomas was out of favour with the craftsmen.

Passing into the nave, the full splendour of Dorchester Abbey is revealed right down to the fourteenth-century east windows that fill the chancel with a kaleidoscope of light and colour. The stained glass, some of it originating in France and Rhineland in the late twelfth century, has lost nothing of its brilliance over hundreds of years, and fills the massive east window, with its saints and Biblical scenes, the world famous Jessie window in the north wall of the sanctuary, and the crests and shields of the families who paid for it all in the window opposite. We could describe these windows in the most meticulous detail and still not be able to convey the splendour born of that unique interaction of sand, pigment and light. The Jessie window itself is an unmatched combination of tracery, sculpture and stained glass figures, showing Jessie, the father of David, with the family tree rising from his recumbent figure, a masterpiece probably without parallel in England. Already damaged in the Civil War, it is no surprise that during the Second World War it was dismantled for fear of damage, or worse, as a result of bombing.

Add some sound, perhaps, and the image is complete. As well as its normal parish functions, the abbey is much sought after as a venue especially for musical events, having been dubbed, 'the best concert venue in Oxfordshire'[114] because of its remarkable acoustic. What could be better, even for the passer-by, with the river flowing gently by, and the strains of some sacred baroque chorale floating across the meadows? Yet the river has witnessed less peaceful times, for Dorchester was visited frequently by troops of both sides during the Civil War, when doubtless different sounds rang out across the river. Once again, the boundary formed by even a relatively small river such as the Thame presented logistical problems to exercise military minds.

Dorchester has been known by a variety of names: Caer Dauri, Caer Dorin, Civitas, Dorciccaestrae, Dorcinia, and Hydropolis among them, the latter being a name contrived by Leland. A common root to all these names is a Latin or old English word meaning water, and Dorchester has long held certain significance because of its strategic location near to a crossing point of the Thames. We should remind ourselves, of course, without wishing to appear overly smug, that Dorchester is to be found on the Thame, but only near the Thames. The present village was built over an important administrative Roman walled town on the Roman road from Silchester to Alchester. Later it became a significant stopping point on the route from London to the West Country, and as a consequence, the village enjoyed a degree of prosperity derived from its coaching trade. Two of the old coaching inns, the George and the White Hart, remain to this day, but it was largely as a result of the wear and tear from this coaching traffic that the old bridge across the River Thame was demolished in 1816, having been replaced by the present structure built shortly before, in 1813-1815. Near the bridge is a small tollhouse, for the main road through the village was one of the county's first turnpike roads.

The earliest reference to a bridge over the Thame at Dorchester is in 1146, though it seems likely from other evidence that there was some crossing arrangement in Anglo-Saxon times. In Leland's era:

> the bridge of archid stone at Dorchester is but a new thinge to speke of'.[115]

He described it as, 'a very faire bridge of stone a little witoute the tonne. The bridg is of a good length: and a great stone causey is made to cum welle onto it. There be 5 principle arches in the bridge, and in the causey joining to the south ende of it.' The structure probably dated from the time of Edward III, but by early 1800, the bridge, 'a mean and narrow structure ... with recesses on the one side to enable foot passengers to avoid the real danger threatened by the transit of carriages' [116] was considered beyond repair, and the present structure built 100 yards above the then existing bridge. For some years after the bridge's demolition in 1816, the piers' foundations remained a potential hazard for river traffic when the water was at a particularly low level.

The new bridge, designed by Francis Sandys, is not surprisingly the largest we have encountered across the Thame, being in total, with its causeways, a remarkable 400-yards long. The main bridge is about seventy-four-feet long, with a single large, capacious central arch, with a smaller arch and still smaller flood arches on either side. The central arch has balustraded parapets, originally with seats that were 'sloped up' in 1847 'so that no person can stand or sit on them'.[117] This seemingly curious modification was made in response to a complaint from some of the ladies in the village who were concerned about the 'nuisances' committed on them that were a disgrace to the parish. The 'slopes' were later removed, but their location can still be made out on the stonework.

Dorchester Bridge, date unknown.

Sandys, incidentally, was responsible for designing a number of diverse, but significant buildings round the country. Perhaps his most famous legacy is Ickworth House in Suffolk, a project on which he collaborated with his brother, Revd Joseph Sandys, on behalf of the genial, but rather eccentric Frederick Augustus Hervey, who was both 4th Earl of Bristol and Bishop of Derry. The wooded parkland around the house was created in part by Lancelot 'Capability' Brown, well remembered for his landscaped garden designs around the country (locally for example, at Blenheim lake, and further afield, Chatsworth park), and now also appreciated as owner of a name with enormous potential to cryptic crossword compilers. Less well known was Brown's involvement in the transformation of the Park at Rycote in 1778, re-landscaping the park and extending medieval fishponds to form the thirteen-acre serpentine lake.

The pre-terminal convolutions of the Thame continue regardless, as oblivious to any contemporary nuisances as it was to the affronted sensitivities of Dorchester's Victorian womenfolk, and as it leaves the historic village behind, the river passes some curious, and even older, earthworks to its right.

The area known as Dyke Hills is interesting on two counts. First is its intrinsic archaeological significance. The remarkable earthworks here are thought to be the remains of an Iron-Age promontory fort and suspected oppidum, a precursor of Roman Dorchester. The double earthworks would have provided defences for the settlement that was protected from all other directions by the River Thame and River Thames. This is, of course, rather speculative. The area includes evidence of an early Saxon burial site, that of a man in uniform with belt fittings consistent with

Dorchester Abbey, seen from the bridge. Note balustrades and evidence of former 'sloping up' of the seats.

those of a Germanic mercenary, and other sites nearby also have revealed Germanic artefacts. Crop marks indicate, to the experts, that the area was at one time quite densely settled, but doubtless we will never know its true significance, and this thought brings us to the second, albeit related, point of interest.

The area has become something of a political pawn in a row that has rumbled on for a hundred years or so. In 1870, Lt-Gen. Augustus Pitt Rivers (1827-1900), a dedicated ethnologist and archaeologist and probably the first to appreciate seriously the importance of the 'ordinary' as opposed to beautiful or valuable archaeological finds, was horrified by the destruction of the ancient ramparts at Dyke Hills that was occurring in the superficially innocent process of converting pasture to arable land. Claiming that the alteration of land from pasture to arable for profit was 'a sordid motive', and suggesting that 'the harmless sheep is no foe to history',[118] he launched a campaign that led eventually to Sir John Lubbock's Ancient Monument Act of 1882. Lubbock, an anthropologist as well as a parliamentarian, later married Pitt Rivers' daughter Alice, so it was clearly a fruitful association all round, though sadly the Act itself did not have the desired or lasting impact its backers desired. Around the same time, photographer Henry Taunt, himself an Oxford man, also bemoaned the destruction of such sites. He observed that the earthworks, 'have been levelled by the farmer who owned the land; but enough is still left to show the immense extent they cover, and create a wonder as to who were the people who carried out such a stupendous system of fortification'.[119] The wonder today is that even recently, Dyke Hills was still being ploughed, and the campaign continues to save such sites from this irrevocable demolition.

Ahead now are the slopes of Little Wittenham Woods and beyond are the rather steeper inclines of the Sinodun Hills and the distinctive skyline of Castle Hill and Round Hill, the Wittenham Clumps. Other colloquial names for this well-known beauty spot include the Berkshire Bubs and Mother Dunch's Buttocks, the latter perhaps being a none too flattering reference to a member of the influential family of local landowners we encountered a little earlier. One of the female members of the Dunch dynasty was Oliver Cromwell's aunt, who, if only by association, may not have been universally popular, and so could be the Mother Dunch thus immortalised. The Dunch family at one time owned much of the land here, and around 1730, it was they that originally planted the ornamental hilltop beeches that with suitable management have continued to dominate the landscape to this day. It was to be the family's parting legacy to the area, for by this time, Edmund Dunch IV, the last male of the dynasty, had died, and by the end of the century, the family's manor house had fallen into a state of decay that soon necessitated complete demolition of the property.

One of the trees at the eastern end of the Clumps' Castle Hill has achieved fame in its own right, for on it was carved in 1844 by Joseph Tubb, a twenty-line poetic meditation on the beauty of nature and the frailty of human ambition. The weird characters are now scarcely recognisable as words, but the full text is recorded on a commemorative stone nearby.

In our times, the Wittenham Clumps form part of the Little Wittenham Nature reserve, an area that includes mixed habitats of grassland, woods, wetland and riverbank. A century ago, the keen-eyed naturalist would have been able to spot polecats and otters here. Sadly, they are no longer to be seen, but the reserve still boasts an interesting mix of flora and fauna, including one of the country's largest populations of a declining species, the great-crested newt. This nocturnal creature, now protected under the 1981 Wildlife and Countryside Act, divides its time between secluded ponds and shady woodland, hiding on land during the day in burrows or under logs, stones and vegetation, and hibernating between October and late February, again, usually, under piles of leaves or logs, or inside hollow tree stumps. It has a characteristic yellow underside, the pattern on each newt being an unique 'fingerprint'.

Great crested newts can live over twenty-five years, and are known to return annually to the same breeding grounds. How many generations have bred here? What stories could the forebears of these little fellows tell? Their pond homes here probably date back to the mid-eighteenth century. Human habitation or utilisation of the hills dates back to Iron-Age Britain and maybe beyond. Flints dating back to the Neolithic era have been found around Castle Hill, almost within the shadow of Didcot's incessant plumes of smoke, a curious juxtaposition of the contrasting extremes of ancient and modern technologies. It seems possible that the ancient Atrebati built a fort on Castle Hill to defend themselves against Caesar's armies – it is surrounded by a deep ditch and ramparts, and has the advantage of a good view

Foot bridge at the confluence of the Thame with the River Thames.

over the surrounding countryside. King Offa of Mercia likewise made use of this vantage point when he built a look-out post on Sinodun, after he had defeated Cynwulf and the Wessex Saxons on the flat land between Warborough and Benson at the Battle of Benson in AD 772.

Overseen by these landmarks of antiquity, the River Thame curls down to join the Thames, about a quarter of a mile south of Dorchester, with, 'a final flourish of a bend, like an extravagant royal signature'.[120] In many ways, the actual confluence, just after a little footbridge over the Thame, is a rather inauspicious, almost unsatisfactory, conclusion to our journey, and the physical, natural and social history that the river has engendered and sustained might seem deserving of something a little more noteworthy. It is a pleasant spot, nonetheless, where swans glide with characteristic imperial poise, moorhens scuttle nervously among the riverside reeds and rushes, and in summer, blue and orange-brown coloured dragonflies skim the banks and banded damselflies the lily pads. Perhaps such an end is in keeping with the character of our gently flowing river, and just as its own little tributaries 'very privately their tribute bring',[121] so the Thame feeds into the greater river unheralded and with modesty. As we saw earlier, the early English poets made much of this union; Leland was more matter of fact, 'Tame and Isis metith aboute half a mile beneathe Dorchestre bridg in the meadowis'.[122] Nature recognises the transition: a yard or so past the footbridge, a low-arched metal structure with sturdy wooden railings and decking, the clumps of yellow water lily that have been much in evidence along the latter miles of the river, disappear abruptly as the character of the water changes, from gentle Thame to faster-flowing Thames.

We can console ourselves with the thought that simplistically, any watercourse, whether Thame, or Thames, or Avon or Amazon, is only as great as the sum of its constituent parts, and each is a microcosm of some greater system. Certainly it is not inappropriate that the River Thame should come to an end at this particular spot, for the Sinodun Hills that overlook its confluence with the Thames are an outcrop of the same chalk deposits that form the hills in which our river rose. Old Chiltern's son has run his course.

nine

Walking Tour

The Thame is intermittently accompanied and crossed by numerous footpaths as it winds its way from the Chilterns to Dorchester. One series of paths offers an almost continuous route from Aylesbury to the mid-point of the river's length, and much of this has been adopted as the Thame Valley Walk (TVW). The walk commences at the end of Rabans Lane, off the A41 road in Aylesbury, and follows a route clearly indicated by signs and arrows. The route described here is based on the Thame Valley Walk, together with suggested alternatives and additions.

The first mile of the walk passes through characteristic rural countryside, before the River Thame is reached at a point where it briefly divides. The walk at this stage coincides with the Midshires Way and the North Bucks Way, and after about a quarter of a mile reaches Weir Lodge, the easternmost property of the Eythrope Estate. After crossing the weir bridge, the footpath follows the original course of the river, with Burn Hill to the left, and through the trees, glimpses of the lake and Eythrope Pavilion to the right.

A right turn onto the metalled road, leads to a bridge, with a waterfall immediately on the right hand side, and continues towards Bridge Lodge. The TVW takes a left turn, as the North Bucks Way follows the road to the right. The footpath, across meadows alongside the more northerly branch of the river, passes the site of an old rectangular moat. Shortly after this the two rivers combine, and soon the footpath turns away from the river, passing the remains of a medieval fishpond adjacent to the river.

A quarter of a mile further on, the path again comes closer to the river, and for a while follows a track lined by pollarded black poplars. Soon the path passes the site of the old mill at Winchendon and then, leaving the river again, continues along the road at the edge of the grounds of Nether Winchendon House. Nether or Lower Winchendon is a delightful village with a good number of picturesque timbered and thatched cottages, some still showing the ochre wash that denotes ownership by the Nether Winchendon estate. Note the curious Victorian letterbox on the little green in sight of the church.

The TVW follows the road to the left. The more adventurous may wish to take a diversion, following part of the Cuddington 'circular' walk to the left, just past the Manor Farm on the right. A series of footpaths leads to Cuddington Mill Farm, a most tranquil spot, and then on to rejoin the TVW about a quarter of a mile from Chearsley. (A good map is recommended for this diversion!)

Starting point of the Thame Valley Walk, by Bear Brook, near Rabans Lane Industrial area, Aylesbury.

In Chearsley village are the tile-topped walls and houses with rounded walls typical of witchert construction. The route skirts around the south of the village, but a footpath to the left tracks back to the river south-east of the church and close to another moat. The TVW, meanwhile, leaves the village, crossing the railway line, and heading towards Notley. A left turn at the prominent dovecote returns the walk, after tantalising glimpses of the abbey, back briefly to the river, before footbridges over the river and old mill stream mark the start of a climb up towards Long Crendon.

St Mary's church dates back to the fifteenth century, and the nearby Court House to the sixteenth century or earlier. There are many other splendid buildings, and the village is well-worth exploring. Long Crendon, from the early fifteenth century, was a major centre for needle making as a cottage industry, and a number of the older houses retain the large windows once needed to give extra light to the needle makers. With its assortment of public houses, the village is perhaps a convenient point to rest and take some refreshment.

The TVW now follows the footpath alongside the road towards Thame. Shortly past the golf range, it leaves the main road, taking the old road past Mead Farm. Just before this road reaches the bypass, the walk turns right along a three-mile footpath across initially low-lying meadows towards the Long Crendon to Shabbington road. Those wishing to explore Thame itself should continue carefully across the bypass, over Crendon Bridge towards the church, and thence into the town.

Instead of following the official TVW towards Thame, some may prefer to follow the road from Long Crendon towards Shabbington. Caution is required as there is no footpath. After about a mile, the TVW joins from the left and soon the footpath leaves the road, taking a rather more direct course that rejoins the road close to the church. Walking away from the village towards Thame, our route goes past the restaurant and the two nearby bridges before striking right across the fields, following the river as it turns south towards the Thame to Oxford A418 road.

From Shabbington, it is possible to follow a network of footpaths out of the village across the fields towards Ickford Bridge and thence to Waterstock. A good map is again recommended for the uninitiated!

Close to the A418, the walk leaves the river, crosses the busy road, with opportunity to take a worthwhile detour to Rycote chapel. The TVW, meanwhile, has joined the Oxfordshire Way, and heads towards the little hamlet of Albury and on to Tiddington. The route loops back up to the often busy A418 and requires that we walk west a hundred yards or so along the verge before the Oxfordshire Way cuts across the fields to the right towards Waterstock. Once through the village, a right turn leads to Waterstock Mill and Bow Bridge, before a straight half mile or so walk into Waterperry, with its church and pleasant and peaceful riverside walk.

Subsequent sections of the river are visible and occasionally enjoy public access, but there is sadly no continuous or contiguous footpath.

References

[1] Holinshed, in *Holinshed's Chronicles '... of Englande, Scotlande and Irelande'* (1965 edition)
[2] Camden, from http://www.philological.bham.ac.uk/campoems/intro.html
[3] Camden, from http://www.genoot.com/eng/oxf/camden.html
[4] Spenser, in *The Faber Book of Poems and Places* (1980)
[5] Drayton, in *The Thames Valley Heritage Walk* (1980)
[6] From http://www.luminarium.org/renlit/idea32.htm
[7] Camden, from http://www.genoot.co.uk/eng/oxf/Camden.html (Translation of *Britannia* by Edmund Gibson 1722)
[8] Taylor, in *Travels through Stuart Britain. The adventures of John Taylor, the Water Poet* (1999)
[9] Taylor, op. cit.
[10] Taylor, *op. cit*
[11] From http://www.icons.org.uk/theicons/collection/holbein/biography/court-artists
[12] Walton, in *The Compleat Angler* (2000 edition)
[13] Walton, *op. cit*
[14] Prior, from www.austen.com/persuade/notes/prior2.htm
[15] Pope, from www.poemhunter.co/alexander-pope/poems/poet-3095/page-2/
[16] Pope, in Alexander Pope Selected Poetry (1998)
[17] Defoe, in *Writings on Travel, Discovery and History by Daniel Defoe* (2001 edition)
[18] Peel, *Buckinghamshire Footpaths* (1949)
[19] Leland, *in The Itinerary of John Leland Parts I-III (1964 edition)*
[20] Defoe, *op. cit*
[21] Rackham, *The History of the Countryside* (1995)
[22] Wright, Francis (1642), in *Chiltern Images* (Read and Empringham 1992)
[23] Mee, *The King's England: Buckinghamshire (1965)*
[24] Leland, *op. cit.*
[25] From http://www.tudorplace.com.ar/WYATT.htm
[26] From http://en.wikipedia.org/wiki/Margaret_Lee
[27] From www.rhymes.org.uk/london-bridge-is-broken-down.htm
[28] From http://www.armoursandbrasiers.co.uk/history_hall.htm#
[29] Beadsman: archaic, meaning 'one who prays for another's soul'
[30] From http://www.poemhunter.com/p/m/poem.asp?poem=36772&poet=6934&num=7
[31] Quoted in Everson, *Quarrendon Aylesbury Vale Buckinghamshire* (1999)
[32] Betjeman (1970), quoted in Haig (Ed), *Country Like This* (1972)
[33] Peel, *op. cit.*
[34] From www.aylesburyvaledc.gov.uk/avdc/get//assets/docs/wh_dev_brief_revs.pdf
[35] From www.aylesburyvaledc.gov.uk/avdc/get//assets/docs/Berryfields4.pdf
[36] Shaw, Marianne, 'History or Debris' in *The Bucks Herald* Wednesday 5th July 2006
[37] William Cobbett (1829), quoted in Haig (Ed), *op. cit.*
[38] Leland, *op. cit.*
[39] Holinshed, *op. cit.*
[40] Leland, *op. cit.*
[41] Leland, *op. cit.*
[42] From www.themodernantiquarian.com/user/1715
[43] From met.open.ac.uk/genuki/big/eng/BKM/waddesdon/index.html
[44] From http://www.startlearningnow.com/articles/Eythrope.htm
[45] From www.canoeist.co.uk/gliders/River%20Thame.doc
[46] Leland, *op. cit.*

[47] From http://www.gallowaykitetrail.com/ gallowaykitetrail/redkitebooks.html
[48] From www.shakespeare-literature.com/Coriolanus/21.html
[49] From http://en.wikiquote.org/wiki/John_Milton
[50] From http://www.bbc.co.uk/threecounties/content/articles/2005/09/07/great_outdoors_bucks_kites_feature.shtml
[51] From http://www.gallowaykitetrail.com/gallowaykitetrail/redkitebooks.html
[52] From http://www.photoaspects.com/chesil/clare/september.html
[53] From www.daypoems.net/poems/1996.html
[54] From http://www.gutenberg.org/dirs/etext05/7pmcl10.txt
[55] Drabble (Ed), in *The Oxford Companion to English Literature* (1985)
[56] Shakespeare, *King Richard II* Act 1, Scene i
[57] Camden, *op. cit.*
[58] Leland, *op. cit.*
[59] Lupton, *The History of Thame and its Hamlets* (1860)
[60] From http://users.ox.ac.uk/~peter/workhouse/Thame/shtml
[61] Mee, *The King's England: Oxfordshire* (1965)
[62] Anderson, *The Upper Thames* (1974)
[63] Camden, in *A Short History of Thame School* (Howard Brown 1927)
[64] From http://www.oldtamensians.co.uk/thepast.html
[65] From http://www.berkshirehistory.com/bios/wlenthall.html
[66] Cull, *Portrait of the Chilterns* (1982)
[67] Pepys, *The Diary of Samuel Pepys Vols 1-3* (1975 edition)
[68] Wood, quoted in http://www.rcplondon.ac.uk/heritage/munksroll/munk_details.asp?ID=5094
[69] Wood, in *A Short History of Thame School* (Howard Brown, 1927)
[70] Wood, in Howard Brown, *op. cit.*
[71] From www.ngfl.ac.uk/tudorhistory/cranmer.html
[72] Wood, in Howard Brown, *op. cit*
[73] Wood, in Howard Brown, *op. cit.*
[74] Ellwood, in Howard Brown, *op. cit.*
[75] *Ibid*
[76] From www.miltonscottage.org
[77] From http://en.wikipedia.org/wiki/John_Wilkes
[78] From http://www.luminariu.org/sevenlit/waller/wallerbio.htm
[79] From http://www.johnhampden.org/name.htm
[80] From Read and Empringham, *op. cit.*
[81] Cull, *op. cit.*
[82] Cannan, *Oxfordshire* (1975)
[83] Hawes, *The Bucks Village Boy* (1994)
[84] In Hayman and Burton, *The Birdlife of Britain (1976)*
[85] Lupton, *op. cit.*
[86] Anon, 'Pupils get hooked on angling' *Thame Gazette* 26 May 2006.
[87] In Read and Empringham, op. cit.
[88] From http://www.foxtalbot.arts.gla.ac.uk/corresp/02864.asp?target=15
[89] Shakespeare, *A Midsummer Night's Dream* Act 2, Scene i
[90] From http://www.ukattraction.com/southern-england/waterperry-church-of-st-mary-the-virgin.htm
[91] From http://www.johnhampden.org/name.htm
[92] Steel, J in www.thisislimitededition.co.uk/ item.asp?category=Country&ID=410
[93] From http://www.defence-estates.mod.uk/conservation_enviro/sanctuary/sanctuary_issue28/otmoor.htm
[94] In Yurdan, *Oxfordshire and Oxford* (1988)
[95] From http://thisislimitededition.co.uk/item.asp?category=Country&ID=801
[96] Leland, *op. cit.*
[97] Wood, in Howard Brown, *op. cit.*
[98] From http://www.scothistoryonline.co.uk/bridges/index.htm
[99] In Maré, *Bridges of Britain* (1975)
[100] Davies, *A Walk along the Thames Path* (1989)
[101] Peel, *op. cit.*
[102] Leland, *op. cit.*
[103] From http://uk.geocities.com/david.hemming1@btinternet.com/characters.htm
[104] From http://www.britainexpress.com/History/bio/pugin.htm

[105] From http://www.wargrave.net/history/mayoo.html
[106] Lobel, *The Victoria History of the Counties of England Volume VII Dorchester and Thame Hundreds* (1962)
[107] Leland, *op. cit.*
[108] From www.berkshirehistory.com/bios/edunch.html quoting a pamphlet from 1660 entitled *'The Mysteries of the Good Old Cause'*
[109] From http://www.dorchester-abbey.org.uk/history.htm
[110] Camden, *op. cit.*
[111] Anderson, *The Regions of Britain: The Upper Thames* (1974)
[112] From http://www.projects.ex.ac.uk/trol/grol/jerome/3men18.htm
[113] Rimmer, *Pleasant Spots around Oxford* (1985)
[114] From http://www.thisislimitededition.co.uk/Item.asp?Category=History&ID=384
[115] Leland, *op. cit*
[116] Lobel, op. cit.
[117] Lobel, op. cit.
[118] Kennedy, Maev, Farmers wrecking ancient sites *The Guardian* 26 July 2003
[119] Read, *The Thames of Henry Taunt* (1989)
[120] Davies, *op. cit.*
[121] Taylor, *op. cit.*
[122] Leland, *op. cit.*

Bibliography

Anderson, J.R.L., *The Regions of Britain: The Upper Thames*
(Eyre Methuen: London, 1974)

Bloxham, Christine, *Folklore of Oxfordshire*
(Tempus: Stroud, 2005)

Bloxham, Christine, *Portrait of Oxfordshire*
(Robert Hale: London, 1982)

Brown, J. Howard, *A Short History of Thame School*
(Hazell Watson & Viney Ltd: London, 1927)

Brown, J. Howard, & Guest, William, *A History of Thame*
(F.H. Castle & Co.: Thame, 1935)

Camp, John, *Portrait of Buckinghamshire*
(Robert Hale: London, 1972)

Cannan, Joanna, *Oxfordshire*
(Robert Hale Ltd: London, 1975)

Chandler, John (Ed), *Travels through Stuart Britain. The adventures of John Taylor, the Water Poet*
(Sutton Publishing: Thrupp, 1999)

Cull, Elizabeth, *Portrait of the Chilterns*
(Robert Hale: London, 1982)

Davies, Gareth Huw, *A Walk along the Thames Path*
(Michael Joseph: London, 1989)

Dickson, Annan, Country of the Thames
(Chaterson Ltd: London, 1948)

Ekwall, Eilert, *The Concise Oxford Dictionary of English Place Names*
(Clarendon Press: Oxford, 1960)

Ekwall, Eilert, *English River Names*
(Clarendon Press: Oxford, 1968)

Everson, P., *Quarrendon Aylesbury Vale Buckinghamshire*
(English Heritage [National Monuments Record]: Swindon, 1999)

Foreman, Wilfred, *Oxfordshire Mills*
(Phillimore & Co. Ltd: Chichester, Sussex, 1983)

Fraser, Mawell, *Companion into Buckinghamshire*
(Methuen & Co.: London, 1950)

Gulland, Peter and Diana, *The Vale of Aylesbury Walker*
(Ramblers Association: London, 1989)

Hammond, Nigel, *The Oxfordshire Village Book*
(Countryside Books: Newbury, 1983)

Haig, Mary Ellen (Ed), *Country Like This*
(Friends of the Vale of Aylesbury: Aylesbury, 1972)

Harries, John, *Discovering Churches*
(Shire Publications: Princes Risborough, 1972)

Hayman, Peter, and Burton, Philip, *The Birdlife of Britain*
(Michael Beazley Publishers: London, 1976)

Holinshed, Raphael and others, *Holinshed's Chronicles of England, Scotland and Ireland,* 1587 edition.
Reprinted London: J. Johnson 1807
(Facsimile reprint AMS Press Inc: New York, 1965)

Hood, Nancy, *Thame to Watlington in Old Photographs*
(Alan Sutton Publishing Ltd: Stroud, 1993)

Inman, H.T., *Near Oxford*
(Alden & Co. Ltd: Oxford, 1948)

Jenkins, Alan, *The Book of the Thames*
(Macmillan: London, 1983)

Jervoise, E., *The Ancient Bridges of Mid and Eastern England*
(Architecture Press: Westminster, 1932)

Kurlansky, Mark, *Salt: A World History*
(Jonathan Cape Ltd: London, 2002)

Lethbridge, Richard, *Oxfordshire and Berkshire (New Shell Guide)*
(Series Ed: John Julius Norwich)
(Michael Joseph Ltd: London, 1988)

Lobel, M.D. (Ed), *The Victoria History of the Counties of England Volume V Bullingdon Hundred* (Series Ed: R.B. Pugh)
(OUP: London, 1957)

Lobel, M. D. (Ed), *The Victoria History of the Counties of England Volume VII Dorchester and Thame Hundred* (Series Ed: R.B. Pugh)
(OUP: London, 1962)

Lupton, Harry, *The History of Thame and its Hamlets*
(Bradford: Thame, 1860)

Maré, Eric de, *Bridges of Britain*
(B.T. Batsford Ltd: London, 1975)

Mee, Arthur (Ed), *The King's England: Buckinghamshire*
(Hodder & Stoughton: London, 1965)

Mee, Arthur (Ed), *The King's England: Oxfordshire*
(Hodder & Stoughton: London, 1965)

Muir, Richard, *Reading the Landscape (Shell Guide)*
(Michael Joseph: London, 1989)

Muir, Richard and Nina, *Rivers of Britain*
(Webb & Bower (Publishers) Ltd: Exeter, 1986)

Page, W. (Ed), *The Victoria History of the Counties of England Volume II Buckingham Hundred* (Series Ed: R.B. Pugh)
(Constable: London, 1908)

Peel, J.H.B., *Buckinghamshire Footpaths*
(Chaterson: London, 1949)

Rackham, Oliver, *The History of the Countryside*
(Weidenfeld & Nicolson: London, 1995)

Read, Susan (Ed), *The Thames of Henry Taunt*
(Alan Sutton Publishing Ltd: Gloucester, 1989)

Read, Susan, and Empringham, David, *Chiltern Images*
(Alan Sutton Publishing Ltd: Stroud, 1992)

Reed, Michael, *The Making of the English Landscape*
(Series Ed: W.G. Hoskins & Roy Millward)
(Hodder & Stoughton: London, 1979)

Rimmer, Alfred, *Pleasant Spots around Oxford*
(reprinted from 1878 edition)
(Thornton & Son: Oxford, 1985)

Rodwell, Kirsty, *Historic Towns in Oxfordshire*
(Oxfordshire Archaeological Unit: Oxford, 1974)

Sherwood, Jennifer, and Pevsner, Nikolaus, *The Bridges of England: Oxfordshire*
(Series Eds: N. Pevsner and J. Nairn)
(Penguin: Harmondsworth, Middlesex, 1974)

Taverner, Eric, *Introduction to Angling*
(Seeley Service & Co: London, 1953)

Tollitt Report on Oxfordshire County Bridges (1878)

Toulmin Smith, Lucy (Ed), *The Itinerary of John Leland Parts I-III*
(Centaur Press: London, 1964)

Walters, Norman, *Thame in old Picture Postcards* (3RD edition)
(European Library: Zaltbommel, 1988)

Warrington, John (Ed), *The Diary of Samuel Pepys Vols 1-3*
(Dent: London, 1906)

Watkin, Bruce, *Buckinghamshire* (Shell Guide)
(Faber & Faber: London, 1981)

Yurdan, Marilyn, *The Changing Face of Thame*
(Robert Boyd Publications: Witney, 2006)

Yurdan, Marilyn, *Discovering Literary Oxfordshire*
(The Book Castle: Dunstable, 2003)

Yurdan, Marilyn, *Oxfordshire and Oxford* (Shire County Guides)
(Shire Publications Ltd: Princes Risborough, 1988)

Index

Alexander, Bishop of Lincoln, 54, 107
Ashurst family, 81, 82
Aston Abbotts, 24, 30
Aylesbury, 11, 13, 19, 20, 23 - 34, 36, 38, 46, 51, 66, 68, 93, 117 - 118
Baldon Brook, 100
Balfour, William, 25 - 26
Bear Brook, 33, 118
Beauforest, Richard, 102, 105, 108
Bernwood Forest, 73, 77, 83
Bigg, John, 65
Birinius, Saint, 107
Black Death, 43, 58
Black poplar, 34, 38, 43, 59, 107, 109, 117
Bolebec, Walter de, 30 - 31
Bow Bridge, 80 - 81, 119
Brill, 34, 73, 77
Brown, Lancelot 'Capability', 112
Buck Pool, 105 - 108
Burn Hill, 34, 117
Burston, 24, 40
Camden, William, 9, 11, 13 - 14, 52, 62 - 63, 77, 107
Camoys, Thomas de, 99
Castle Hill, 114
Chalgrove, 97 - 98
Charles I, 64 - 65, 68, 75 - 76, 86, 90
Charles II, 65, 68
Chearsley, 41, 43 - 44, 117 - 118
Cheddington, 20 - 22
Chiltern Hills, 10 - 11, 13, 16, 19 - 20, 33 - 34, 36, 49, 51, 55, 59, 93, 116 - 117
Chippinghurst, 94 - 95
Chiselhampton, 10, 68, 95 - 97, 99, 100
Churches
St Catherine and St Leonard, Drayton St Leonard, 103
St Glen, Newington, 101
St Katherine, Chiselhampton, 96 - 97
St Laurence, Warborough, 109
St Lawrence, Rowsham, 24
St Leonard Waterstock, 81
St Mary, Long Wittenham, 109
St Mary, Thame, 53, 60 - 61, 63
St Mary the Virgin, Waterperry, 79
St Mary Magdalene, Shabbington, 72
St Nicholas, Chearsley, 43
St Nicholas, Cuddington, 42
St Nicholas, Ickford, 77
St Nicholas, Nether Winchendon, 39 - 40
St Peter, Quarrendon, 28
Civil War, 14, 25 - 26, 30, 61 - 62, 66 - 69, 77, 84, 86, 93, 97, 102, 109 - 110
Coutances, Walter de, 56
Cranmer, Thomas, 66
Creslow, 30
Croke, George, 82
Cromwell, Oliver, 15, 26, 30, 65, 68, 83, 101, 109, 114
Cublington, 30
Cuddesdon, 10, 49, 90 - 91, 93 - 95
Cuddington, 38, 41 - 44, 53, 117
Cuddington Mill, 41 - 42, 117
Curson family, 80
Cuttle Brook, 51 - 52, 55, 115
Cuxham Brook, 99
Dadbrook, 44
D'Alderby, John, 53, 56
Defoe, Daniel, 17 - 19
Dinton Hermit, 65
Domesday Book, 20, 28, 31, 36 - 39, 41, 50, 56, 73, 75, 81, 87, 94, 105, 107
Dormer family, 36, 62
Dorchester, 10 - 12, 14 - 16, 18, 43, 45, 49, 55 - 56, 72, 97, 102 - 103, 105, 107 - 113, 115, 117
D'Oyley family, 95 - 96, 99
Drayton, Michael, 9, 13 - 14
Drayton St Leonards, 101 - 105
Dunch family, 101 - 102, 105, 114
Dyke Hills, 112 - 113
Edward I, 56
Edward III, 111
Edward VI, 62
Edward the Confessor, 40, 73 – 74, 77
Edyth, Queen, 40
Elizabeth I, 28 - 29, 40, 58, 62, 75, 90
Ellwood, Thomas, 67
Eythrope, 34 - 36, 38, 117
Fell, John, 65 - 66, 93
Ferguson, William, 93
Figg, James, 69
FitzElys family, 80, 96
Giffard, Walter, 30, 40, 45
Great Holcombe, 101
Grosseteste, Robert, 60 - 61

Haddenham, 10, 41, 50 - 51, 56, 94
Hampden, John, 26, 62, 64, 68 - 69, 82 - 83, 95, 97 - 98
Hardwick, 10, 23, 26, 30 - 31
Haseley Brook, 95
Hayward's Bridge, 103
Henley family, 80
Henry I, 28
Henry II, 56, 73, 85, 94
Henry III, 56, 70
Henry VIII, 28 - 29, 45, 54, 59, 62, 66, 75
Holinshed, Raphael, 9 - 11, 18, 32
Holman's Bridge, 24 - 27, 31 - 32, 41
Holt, John, 67
Holton Brook, 79, 83
Holton Mill, 83
Hucket, 10
Hulcott, 22 - 24
Hurst Water Meadow, 106, 108 - 109
Ickford, 75, 77 - 79, 119
Ingoldsby, Richard, 65
Isis, 11 - 18, 115
James I, 75, 90
James II, 65
Jemmett's Hole, 54, 71
King, Robert, 70
Knolleys family, 40
Laud, William, 85 - 86, 97
Lee family, 23 - 24, 27 - 30, 40, 62, 82
Leland, John, 10 - 11, 19, 21, 27, 32 - 33, 43, 53, 77, 85, 95, 99, 111, 115
Lenthall, William, 64
Long Crendon, 27, 34, 43, 45, 49 - 50, 53, 94, 118 - 119
Long Marston, 31, 33
Lupton, Harry, 63, 75
Lyde Brook, 34, 65
Mandeville, Geoffrey de, 28
Marsworth, 10, 19
Mayne, Simon, 64 - 65
Meadowcroft, 27
Mentmore, 19
Milton Common, 10, 18, 77, 84 - 85, 95
Milton, Great, 90, 99
Milton, Little, 95
Newington, 101 - 103
North Weston, 58, 62, 103
Notley Abbey, 10, 31, 40 - 41, 45 - 47, 49, 58, 118
Nugent, Lord, 26
Ogilby, John, 86 - 87
Oswyth, Saint, 28
Otmoor, 70, 82 - 83
Overy Mill, 105 - 108
Oving, 28
Oxford, 10, 14, 21, 25, 45, 51, 54, 56, 60, 65 - 66, 68 - 70, 73, 75 - 77, 79, 84 - 86, 88 - 89, 93, 96 – 97, 105, 113, 119
Peers, Charles, 96
Pitchcott, 28, 33
Pitt-Rivers, Augustus, 113
Plot, Robert, 69, 76
Pope, Alexander, 17 - 18
Prior, Matthew, 16 - 17
Puttenham, 10
Quarrendon, 23, 27 - 31, 40, 62
Quartermain Richard, 58, 62, 72, 76
Queenford Mill, 105, 107
Remigius, 56, 107
Rothschild family, 35 - 36
Rowsham, 20, 24
Rupert, Prince, 25, 67 - 68, 97
Rycote, 34, 58, 73, 75 - 77, 112, 119
Rycotewood College, 54 - 56
Scotsgrove, 50, 51
Shabbington 10, 71 - 73, 75, 118 - 119
Shakespeare, William, 9, 15, 23, 47 - 48, 51 - 52, 79
Sheldon, Gilbert, 79
Shotover, 84, 89 - 90, 93
Sinodun Hills, 114 - 116
Spencer-Barnard family, 40 - 41
Spenser, Edmund, 11, 13
Stadhampton, 95, 97, 99 - 100, 102 - 103
Stone Bridge, 10, 32 - 33
Stewkley, 30
Stribblehill, 58 - 59
Taunt, Henry, 106, 113
Taylor, John, 9, 14 - 15, 102
Thame, 10, 11, 16, 18 - 19, 41, 49 - 73, 75, 86, 89, 103, 118 - 119
Thame Park, 56, 70
Thame Valley Walk, 34, 117 - 119
Thames, River, 10 - 11, 13 - 14, 16 - 19, 43, 49, 55, 57, 96, 100, 102, 105, 107 - 108, 111 - 112, 115 - 116
Thistlebrook, 19, 21 – 24
Thynne family, 54, 59, 62
Tiscott, 21 - 22
Trotman, Hugh, 56
Vavasour, Anne, 28
Waddesdon Manor, 35, 36
Waller, Edmund, 68
Walton Bridge, 32 - 33
Walton, Izaac, 15 - 16
Watermead, 24 - 25, 31
Waterperry, 49, 79 - 80, 96, 119
Waterstock, 10, 79 - 83, 119
Wenman, Richard, 70
Wheatley, 18, 82 - 90, 97
Whistler, Daniel, 65
Wilkes, John, 67 - 68
William the Conqueror, 20, 30, 56, 107
Williams, John, 58, 62 - 63, 66, 70, 75, 86
Williams's, Lord, School, 64 - 65, 67 - 68, 81, 86
Wilstone, 19
Winchendon, Nether (Lower), 38 - 41, 92, 117
Winchendon Mill, 38 - 39
Wingrave, 24
Wittenham Clumps, 17, 103, 114
Wood, Anthony, 65 - 66, 75
Wyatt, Margaret, 27